PENGUIN BOOKS — GREAT IDEAS

Consolation in the Face of Death

Samuel Johnson

1709–1784

Samuel Johnson

Consolation in the Face of Death

PENGUIN BOOKS — GREAT IDEAS

PENGUIN BOOKS

Published by the Penguin Group
Penguin Books Ltd, 80 Strand, London WC2R ORL, England
Penguin Group (USA) Inc., 375 Hudson Street, New York, New York 10014, USA
Penguin Group (Canada), 90 Eglinton Avenue East, Suite 700, Toronto, Ontario, Canada M4P 2Y3
(a division of Pearson Penguin Canada Inc.)
Penguin Ireland, 25 St Stephen's Green, Dublin 2, Ireland
(a division of Penguin Books Ltd)
Penguin Group (Australia), 250 Camberwell Road, Camberwell, Victoria 3124, Australia
(a division of Pearson Australia Group Pty Ltd)
Penguin Books India Pvt Ltd, 11 Community Centre, Panchsheel Park, New Delhi – 110 017, India
Penguin Group (NZ), 67 Apollo Drive, Rosedale, North Shore 0632, New Zealand
(a division of Pearson New Zealand Ltd)
Penguin Books (South Africa) (Pty) Ltd, 24 Sturdee Avenue,
Rosebank, Johannesburg 2196, South Africa

Penguin Books Ltd, Registered Offices: 80 Strand, London WC2R ORL, England

www.penguin.com

'The State of Affairs in Lilliput' and 'On Gay's Epitaph' first published in 1738
'A Compleat Vindication of the Licensers of the Stage' first published in 1739
'An Essay on Epitaphs' first published in 1740
'The Vision of Theodore, the Hermit of Teneriffe' first published in 1748
'On Theory and Practice' first published in The Rambler No. 14 in 1750
'The Benefits of Human Society' first published in The Adventurer no. 67 in 1753
'The Role of the Scholar' first published in The Adventurer no. 85 in 1753
'Observations on the present State of Affairs' first published in 1756
'Of the Duty of a Journalist' first published in 1758
'The Vultures' View of Man' first published in The Idler no. 22 (original numbering) in 1758
'Debtors' Prisons (I)' first published in The Idler no. 22 (revised numbering) in 1758
'Consolation in the Face of Death' first published in The Idler no. 41 in 1759
'The Nature of a Critic' first published in The Idler no. 60 in 1759
'European Oppression in America' first published in The Idler no. 81 in 1759

This selection first published in Penguin Books 2009

1

All rights reserved

Set by Rowland Phototypesetting Ltd, Bury St Edmunds, Suffolk
Printed in England by Clays Ltd, St Ives plc

978-0-141-04370-8

www.greenpenguin.co.uk

Penguin Books is committed to a sustainable future
for our business, our readers and our planet.
The book in your hands is made from paper
certified by the Forest Stewardship Council.

Contents

The State of Affairs in Lilliput

The public several years ago received a great deal of entertainment and instruction from Capt. Gulliver's elaborate and curious account of the newly discovered empire of Lilliput; a relation which (however rejected at its first appearance by some as incredible, and criticized by others as partial or ostentatious) has, with the success almost always attendant on probity and truth, triumphed over all opposition, gained belief from the most obstinate incredulity and established a reputation in the world which can fear no dimunition, nor admit of any increase.

It is much to be regretted that the ingenious traveller was diverted from his design of completing a full and accurate description of that unknown country, by bringing down its history from the earliest ages, explaining the laws and customs of the inhabitants, and delineating the works of art and productions of nature peculiar to that soil and people. Happy had it been for mankind had so noble and instructive a subject been cultivated and adorned by the genius of LEMUEL GULLIVER, a genius equally sublime and extensive, acute and sagacious, worthy to display the policy of the most refined, and celebrate the achievements of the most warlike nation. Then might the legislators of Lilliput have been produced as rivals in fame to Numa or Lycurgus; and its heroes have shone with no less lustre than Cadmus and Theseus.

Felix tanto argumento ingenium, felix tanto ingenio argumentum! ['Happy is the intellect to which so great a subject is presented; happy is the subject to which so great an intellect is brought.']

But as the hope conceived by the public of seeing this immense undertaking successfully completed has been frustrated by indolence, business, or perhaps by the unexpected stroke of sudden death, we doubt not but our readers will be much pleased with an appendix to Capt. Gulliver's account, which we received last month, and which the late resolution of the House of Commons, whereby we are forbidden to insert any account of the proceedings of the British Parliament, gives us an opportunity of communicating in their room.

Some years after the publication of Capt. Gulliver's discoveries, in the midst of the clamour raised against them by ignorance, misapprehension, and malice, a grandson of the Captain's, fired with resentment at the indignities offered to his ancestor's character by men who, without the least regard to his celebrated veracity, dared to charge his relation with no less than premeditated, deliberate falsehood, resolved, as the most effectual method of vindicating his memory, to undertake a voyage to Lilliput, that he might be able at his return to confirm his grandfather's reports by ocular testimony, and forever silence those aspersions, which were, in his opinion, founded on nothing but extreme ignorance of both geography and human nature.

This voyage, by the assistance of some charts and observations which he found amongst his grandfather's papers, he successfully performed in the ship named the

Confidence, and met, upon his discovering his name and family, with such a reception at the court of Lilliput as sufficiently showed that the memory of the Man-Mountain was far from being obliterated among them; and that time had in Lilliput the effect which it is observed to have on our side of the globe, of preserving and increasing a reputation built on great and illustrious actions, and of dissipating the whispers of malice and calumnies of faction. The accusations brought against the Captain by his enemies were cleared up, or forgot; and the grandson, at his arrival, found the preservation of Mildendo from the flames, and the conquest of the formidable navy of Blefuscu, the subject of epic poems, and annual orations, the old man's constant topic of discourse, and the example by which their youth were animated to fidelity, presence of mind, and military prowess.

The hospitable and generous reception he found in the country gave him opportunities of informing himself more fully of the state of that part of the world; for which he came prepared by his grandfather's conversation, and a tolerable knowledge of the Lilliputian tongue, attained by the help of a grammar and a vocabulary, which, with other writings in that language, Captain Gulliver had left behind him.

Enabled by these concurrent advantages to make a speedy progress in his enquiries, he returned at the end of three years, not with a cargo of gold or silk or diamonds, but with histories, memoirs, tracts, speeches, treaties, debates, letters and instructions, which will be a sufficient compensation to mankind for the loss they have sustained by the negligence or untimely death of Captain Gulliver; and established a correspondence between Lilliput and the English colonies in the East-Indies, by which all the valuable writings published there, and all historical and political novelties, are to be annually transmitted to him.

This gentleman, notwithstanding that veneration for his grandfather which engaged him to take so long and tedious a voyage, upon no other motive than a desire of obliging the world to do justice to his character, has given the highest testimonies that truth is yet dearer to him than the reputation of his family, and that no mistaken piety can prevail upon him to palliate the mistakes, or conceal the errors which were the necessary effects of Capt. Gulliver's short stay, difficult situation, formidable appearance, and perplexed affairs.

The ready access to the great men of Lilliput, and familiarity with the Emperor himself, which the traditional regard paid to his grandfather's merit procured him, rendered it easy for him to make greater discoveries in three days than Capt. Gulliver had been able to do during his whole stay. He was particularly surprised in his first conference with the Emperor, to hear him mention many states and empires beside those of Lilliput and Blefuscu; and, upon observing that in his grandfather's account no other nations are taken notice of, he was told with great condescension by his Majesty that there had been lately discovered, in an old repository of archives, an edict of those times absolutely forbidding, under the pain and penalty of death, any person or persons to give the Man-Mountain the least information relating to the state of any other country; lest his ambition might prompt him to seize upon some defenceless part, either of his Lilliputian majesty's dominions, or of some weak prince, or petty state, and to erect an absolute dominion, which might in time perhaps become formidable to the state of Lilliput itself. 'Nor do I believe', said his Majesty, 'that your ancestor would have heard the name of Blefuscu, had not the necessities of state obliged the court unwillingly to discover it; and even in that emergence of affairs, they gave him so imperfect an account that he has represented Blefuscu as an island; whereas it is a very large empire on the continent, confining on other empires, kingdoms, and states, of which I'll order my geographer to communicate to you an accurate description.'

He had immediately recourse to the royal professor of geography, and found upon inspection that the maps of Lilliput and Blefuscu, and the neighbouring islands, kingdoms, and empires, were a perfect epitome of the map of Europe, and that these petty regions, with their dependencies, constitute a resemblance or compendium of our great world, just as the model of a building contains all the parts in the same disposition as the principal design.

This observation engaged him closely to his geographical studies, and the farther he advanced, the more he was convinced of the justness of the notion he had conceived of a world in miniature, inhabited by this pigmy race. In it he found all the four parts of our earth represented by correspondent countries, excepting that the Lilliputian world is not spherical, but must be considered as bearing the form which the ancients attributed to our own. Neither need I acquaint the mathematical readers that, being enlightened by our sun, it does not admit of any diversity of zones or climates, but bears an exact analogy to our earth in its lands and seas, chains of mountains, tracts of deserts, and diversity of nations.

The people of Degulia, or the Lilliputian Europe, which name is derived from DEGUL, illustrious (a word now obsolete, and known only to antiquaries and etymologists), are, above those of the other parts of the world, famous for arts, arms, and navigation, and, in consequence of this superiority, have made conquests and settled colonies in very distant regions, the inhabitants of which they look upon as barbarous, though in simplicity of manners, probity, and temperance superior to themselves; and seem to think that they have a right to treat them as passion, interest, or caprice shall direct, without much regard to the rules of justice or humanity; they have carried this imaginary sovereignty so far that they have sometimes proceeded to rapine, bloodshed, and desolation. If you endeavour to examine the foundation of this authority, they neither produce any grant from a superior jurisdiction, nor plead the consent of the people whom they govern in this tyrannical manner; but either threaten you with punishment for abridging the Emperor's sovereignty, or pity your stupidity, or tell you in positive terms that *Power is right*. Some indeed pretend to a grant from a pontiff, to whom, as they happen to be inclined, they sometimes pay an absolute submission, and as often deny common respect; but this grant is not worth examination, the pontiff from whom it is derived being equally at a loss to fix his own authority upon any solid ground; so that at best the Degulians' claim to these settlements is like the Mahometan world, which rests upon an elephant, which is supported by a stone, which is supported by nothing.

It is observable that their conquests and acquisitions in Columbia (which is the Lilliputian name for the country that answers our America) have very little contributed to the power of those nations which have, to obtain them, broke through all the ties of human nature. They have indeed added extent to their territories, and procured new titles for their princes, but at the same time have exhausted their mother country of its inhabitants, and subjected themselves to a thousand insults, by possessing vast tracts of land, which are too spacious to be constantly garrisoned, and too remote to be occasionally and duly supplied.

Even Iberia, a country at the southwest point of Degulia, whose inhabitants were the first discoverers of Columbia, though she boasts herself mistress of the richest and most fertile part of that quarter of the world, which she secured to herself by the most dreadful massacres and devastations, has not yet, in all the gold she has imported, received an equivalent for the numbers of her natives sent out to people those kingdoms her sword has wasted; so that the whole advantage of her mighty conquests is bulk without strength, and pride without power.

It must be observed to the honour of the Lilliputians, who have in all ages been famous for their politics, that they have the art of civilizing their remote dominions without doing much injury to their native country; for when any of their people have forfeited the rights of society, by robberies, seditions, or any other crimes which make it not safe to suffer them to live, and yet are esteemed scarce heinous enough to be punished with death, they send them to some distant colony for a certain number of years proportionate to their crimes. Of these Mr Gulliver, during his stay, saw ten thousand conveyed from the prisons of Mildendo in close lighters to ships that lay at anchor in the river to carry them to Columbia, where they were disposed among the inhabitants, undoubtedly very much to the propagation of knowledge and virtue, and no less to the honour of their native country.

Another inconvenience of these new claims is that they are a constant source of discord and debate among the Degulian powers, some of which are perpetually disputing their titles to countries which neither has a right to, and which sometimes are defended by the natives against both. There not long since arose a quarrel of this kind between the Lilliputians and Iberians, who contested the limits of their Columbian (or American) acquisitions. The Lilliputians, contrary to the ancient genius of that martial people, made very liberal concessions, such as rather drew upon them the imputation of cowardice than procured them the praise of moderation; but the Iberians, insatiable in their ambition, resolved to insist on nothing less than the absolute uninterrupted possession of that whole quarter of the world. In pursuance of this resolution they seized, upon various pretences, all the Lilliputian shipping that ventured or were drove near their shores in the Columbian seas, confiscated their lading, and imprisoned, tortured, and starved their seamen. The Lilliputians were patient under all these insults for a long time, but being at length awakened by frequent injuries were making, at Mr Gulliver's departure, preparations for war; the event of which is not yet come to his knowledge.

Our author, having satisfied his curiosity with regard to the geography of this petty world, began to enquire more nearly into the constitution and laws of Lilliput. But how great was his surprise when he found it so nearly to resemble our own! The executive power being lodged wholly in the Emperor; as the legislative is in the Emperor, the House of Hurgoes, or Lords, whose honours and privileges are hereditary, and the House of Clinabs, or Commons, representatives elect of the body of the people, whose assemblies are continued by several sessions and adjournments or prorogations, for the space of seven moons, after which their authority determines, and writs are issued for new elections.

Mr Gulliver, astonished at this wonderful conformity between the constitution of England and Lilliput, consulted Flibo Quibus, the royal historiographer, upon that subject, who gave him the following account:

'Tis now, according to the best chronologers, more than 392 moons since the arrival of your illustrious ancestor Quinbus Flestrin, or the Man-Mountain, upon the confines of Lilliput, where he performed those achievements still recorded in our histories, and celebrated by our poets; but alas! he was at last disgraced and banished by the effects of the most undeserved calumny and malice.

After his departure, the people, who had been irritated against him by false reports, finding the same evil measures that were imputed to his advice still pursued, and all the calamities still subsisting which had been described as the effects of his stay amongst them, were on the sudden not only convinced of his innocence, but so exasperated against his enemies, by the remembrance of his wisdom, clemency, and valour, that they surrounded the royal palace, and demanded the heads of the Man-Mountain's accusers. The ministers, according to custom, ran for shelter to the royal authority; but far from appeasing the people by that artifice, they involved their master in the common destruction.

The people having set fire to the palace, and buried the whole royal family in its ruins, placed one Mulgo Malvin, who had been secretary to the Man-Mountain, upon the throne of Lilliput. This man new-modelled the form of government, according to the plan which his master had delivered to him and affirmed to be an exact account of the British constitution.

Our government [continued the Lilliputian] has in some particulars varied from its original. The Clinabs were at first elected every moon, but now continue in office seven moons; to which alteration many attribute the present venality and dependency discovered in their assemblies. They were likewise anciently paid by the people they represented for their attendance on the public business; but of late it is more common for the Clinabs to pay the people for admitting them to attend. Our ancestors, in ancient times, had some regard to the moral character of the person sent to represent them in their national assemblies, and would have shown some degree of resent-

ment, or indignation, had their votes been asked for a murderer, an adulterer, a known oppressor, an hireling evidence,
an attorney, a gamester, or a pimp. They demanded likewise
in those who stood candidates for the power of making laws
some knowledge of the laws already made; but now neither
the most flagrant immorality, nor the grossest ignorance, are,
amongst some electors, any objections to the character of a
man who solicits voices with gold in his hand.

Such was the answer of the learned Lilliputian which
incited Mr Gulliver to pursue his search into their laws,
customs, and history; if haply he might discover, since
human nature generally operates alike in all parts of
the world, by what means the government of Lilliput,
which had been once established on so excellent a plan,
became so miserably degenerate; while the government
of Britain, its original, maintained inviolate the purity
and vigour of its primitive constitution.

As we propose to publish every month such part of
Mr Gulliver's papers as shall seem most proper to bring
our readers acquainted with the history and present state
of Lilliput, we have chose for this half year's entertainment the debates of the Lilliputian senate, and shall begin
with a very important one upon occasion of the Iberian
depredations already mentioned, and the measures to be
pursued for redress, which debate, as indeed all others
on such high affairs, was carried on with the greatest
eloquence and spirit, in the 4th session of the 8th senate
(or parliament) of Magna Lilliputia, held at Belfaborac in
the 11th moon of the reign of the Emperor Gorgenti the
Second.

On Gay's Epitaph

Mr Urban,
Matters of very small consequence in themselves are often made important by the circumstances that attend them. Little follies and petty weaknesses, of no moment in common life, may, when they enter into the characters of men in high stations, obstruct the happiness of a great part of mankind. A barbarous inscription or dispropor-tioned busto deserves no notice on account of the statu-ary who carved it or the writer who composed it; they were only private follies in the study or the shop; but erected in a temple, or engraved on a column, they are considered as public works, and censured as a disgrace to a nation. For this reason I have been often offended with the trifling distich upon Mr Gay's monument in Westminster Abbey:

> Life is a jest, and all things show it;
> I thought so once, but now I know it.

I never heard when or where this wonderful couplet was composed, or to what happy genius we are indebted for it: the miserable poetry of the first line makes it unlikely that it could be a studied production, unless it were one of the first efforts of a romantic girl, or some dapper school-boy's imitation of

Παντα γελως, και παντα κονις, και παντα το μηδεν.
['All is laughter, all is dust, all is nothingness.']

If I might be indulged in making conjectures on a question of such weight, I should conceive it to have been a drunken sally, which was perhaps, after midnight, applauded as a lively epigram, and might have preserved its reputation had it, instead of being engraved on a monument at Westminster, been scribbled in its proper place, the window of a brothel.

There are very different species of wit appropriated to particular persons and places; the smartness of a shoeboy would not be extremely agreeable in a chancellor, and a tavern joke sounds but ill in a church, from which it ought to be banished, if for no other reason, at least for that which forbids a drunken man to be introduced into sober company.

Yet, lest this epigram should have any secret merit which, though it has escaped the observation of negligent and vulgar readers, has entitled it to the place I have found it in possession of, we will consider it with a little more attention than I fear we shall discover it to deserve.

The design of epitaphs is rational and moral, being generally to celebrate the virtues of the dead, and to excite and awaken the reader to the imitation of those excellencies which he sees thus honoured and distinguished, of which kind almost every sepulchral monument affords us an example.

There is another kind, in which the person departed is represented as delivering some precept to those whom he has left behind him, or uttering some important sentence suitable to his present state, from which the reader is prepared to receive very strong impressions by the silence and solemnity of the place where such inscriptions are generally found, and by the serious and affecting thoughts which naturally arise at the sight of the receptacles of the dead, upon the transitory and uncertain nature of human pleasure, vanity, and greatness. Of this sort the most ancient and the best that I have met with is that ordered (if I forget not) by the great Sesostris to be inscribed on his tomb,

Εις εμε τις οραων, ενσεβης εστω.
Let every man who looks upon me learn to be pious.

On this monument perhaps no man ever looked without being, at least for some time, wiser and better, and doubtless, by so striking an instruction, the libertine has been often checked in the height of his debaucheries, and the oppressor softened in the midst of his tyranny. Perhaps, as long life is often the effect of virtue, the tomb of Sesostris may have more than repaired the ravages of his arms. Of this latter kind is the important distich we are considering. Mr Gay, like the Egyptian king, calls upon us from the habitations of the dead; but in such a manner and for such ends as shows what was anciently believed, that departed souls still preserve the characters they supported on earth, and that the author of the *Beggar's Opera* is not yet on the level with Sesostris. I cannot help thinking upon the dialogue on this occasion between Oedipus and his Jocasta:

Was Laius used to lie?
Joc. O no! the most sincere, plain, honest man; one that abhorred a lie.
Oed. Then he has got that quality in hell.

Dryden

Mr Gay has returned from the regions of death not much improved in his poetry, and very much corrupted in his morals; for he is come back with a lie in his mouth, *Life is a jest*.

Mankind, with regard to their notions of futurity, are divided into two parties: a very small one that believes, or pretends to believe, that the present is the only state of existence; and another, which acknowledges that in some life to come, men will meet rewards or punishments according to their behaviour in this world.

In one of the classes our poet must be ranked: if he properly belonged to the first, he might indeed think life a jest, and might live as if he thought so; but I must leave it to acuter reasoners to explain how he could in that case *know* it after death, being for my part inclined to believe that knowledge ceases with existence.

If he was of the latter opinion, he must think life more than a jest, unless he thought eternity a jest too; and if these were his sentiments, he is by this time most certainly undeceived. These lines, therefore, are impious in the mouth of a Christian, and nonsense in that of an atheist.

But whether we consider them as ludicrous or wicked, they ought not to stand where they are at present; buffoonery appears with a very ill grace, and impiety with much worse, in temples and on tombs. A childish levity has of late infected our conversation and behaviour, but let it not make its way into our churches. Irreligion has corrupted the present age, but let us not inscribe it on marble, to be the ruin or scorn of another generation. Let us have some regard to our reputation amongst foreigners, who do not hold either fools or atheists in high veneration, and will imagine that they can justify themselves in terming us such from our own monuments. Let us therefore review our public edifices, and, where inscriptions like this appear, spare our posterity the trouble of erasing them.

PAMPHILUS.

A Compleat Vindication of the Licensers of the Stage,

FROM THE MALICIOUS AND SCANDALOUS ASPERSIONS OF MR *BROOKE*, AUTHOR OF *Gustavus Vasa* WITH A PROPOSAL FOR MAKING THE OFFICE OF LICENSER MORE EXTENSIVE AND EFFECTUAL. BY AN IMPARTIAL HAND.

It is generally agreed by the Writers of all Parties, that few Crimes are equal, in their Degree of Guilt, to that of calumniating a good and gentle, or defending a wicked and oppressive Administration.

It is therefore with the utmost Satisfaction of Mind, that I reflect how often I have employed my Pen in Vindication of the present Ministry, and their Dependents and Adherents, how often I have detected the specious Fallacies of the Advocates for Independence, how often I have softened the Obstinacy of Patriotism, and how often triumphed over the Clamour of Opposition.

I have, indeed, observed but one Set of Men upon whom all my Arguments have been thrown away, which neither Flattery can draw to Compliance, nor Threats reduce to Submission, and who have, notwithstanding all Expedients that either Invention or Experience could suggest, continued to exert their Abilities in a vigorous and constant Opposition of all our Measures.

The unaccountable Behaviour of these Men, the enthusiastick Resolution with which, after a hundred successive Defeats, they still renewed their Attacks, the Spirit with which they continued to repeat their Arguments in the Senate, though they found a Majority determined to condemn them, and the Inflexibility with which they rejected all Offers of Places and Preferments at last excited my Curiosity so far that I applied myself to enquire with great Diligence into the real Motives of their Conduct, and to discover what Principle it was that had Force to inspire such unextinguishable Zeal, and to animate such unwearied Efforts.

For this Reason I attempted to cultivate a nearer Acquaintance with some of the Chiefs of that Party, and imagined that it would be necessary for some Time to dissemble my Sentiments that I might learn theirs.

Dissimulation to a true Politician is not difficult, and therefore I readily assumed the Character of a Proselyte, but found that their Principle of Action was no other, than that which they make no Scruple of avowing in the most publick Manner, notwithstanding the Contempt and Ridicule to which it every Day exposes them, and the Loss of those Honours and Profits from which it excludes them.

This wild Passion, or Principle, is a kind of Fanaticism by which they distinguish those of their own Party, and which they look upon as a certain Indication of a great Mind. *We* have no name for it *at Court*, but among themselves, they term it by a kind of *Cant-phrase*, A REGARD FOR POSTERITY.

This Passion seems to predominate in all their Conduct, to regulate every Action of their Lives, and Sentiment of their Minds; I have heard *L*— and *P*—, when they have made a vigorous Opposition, or blasted the Blossom of some ministerial Scheme, cry out, in the Height of their Exultations, *This will deserve the Thanks of Posterity!*

And when their Adversaries, as it much more frequently falls out, have out-number'd and overthrown them, they will say with an Air of Revenge, and a kind of gloomy Triumph, *Posterity will curse you for this*.

It is common among Men under the Influence of any kind of Frenzy, to believe that all the World has the same odd Notions that disorder their own Imaginations. Did these unhappy Men, these deluded Patriots, know how little we are concerned about Posterity, they would never attempt to fright us with their Curses, or tempt us to a Neglect of our own Interest by a Prospect of their Gratitude.

But so strong is their Infatuation, that they seem to have forgotten even the primary Law of Self-preservation, for they sacrifice without scruple every flattering Hope, every darling Enjoyment, and every Satisfaction of Life to this *ruling Passion*, and appear in every Step to consult not so much their own Advantage as that of *Posterity*.

Strange Delusion! that can confine all their Thoughts to a Race of Men whom they neither know, nor can know; from whom nothing is to be feared, nor any Thing expected; who cannot even bribe a special Jury, nor have so much as a single Riband to bestow.

This Fondness for Posterity is a kind of Madness which at *Rome* was once almost epidemical, and infected even the Women and the Children. It reigned there till the entire

Destruction of *Carthage*, after which it began to be less general, and in a few Years afterwards a Remedy was discovered, by which it was almost entirely extinguished.

In *England* it never prevailed in any such Degree; some few of the ancient Barons seem indeed to have been disorder'd by it, but the Contagion has been for the most part timely checked, and our Ladies have been generally free.

But there has been in every Age a Set of Men much admired and reverenced, who have affected to be always talking of Posterity, and have laid out their Lives upon the Composition of Poems for the Sake of being applauded by this imaginary Generation.

The present Poets I reckon amongst the most inexorable Enemies of our most excellent Ministry, and much doubt whether any Method will effect the Cure of a Distemper which in this Class of Men may be termed not an accidental Disease, but a Defect in their original Frame and Constitution.

Mr *Brooke*, a Name I mention with all the Detestation suitable to my Character, could not forbear discovering this Depravity of his Mind in his very Prologue, which is filled with Sentiments so wild, and so much unheard of among those who frequent Levees and Courts, that I much doubt, whether the zealous Licenser proceeded any further in his Examination of his Performance.

He might easily perceive that a Man,

Who bade his moral Beam through every Age,

was too much a Bigot to exploded Notions, to compose a Play which he could license without manifest Hazard of his Office, a Hazard which no Man would incur untainted with the Love of Posterity.

We cannot therefore wonder that an Author, wholly possessed by this Passion, should vent his Resentment for the Licenser's just Refusal, in virulent Advertisements, insolent Complaints, and scurrilous Assertions of his Rights and Privileges, and proceed in Defiance of Authority to solicite a Subscription.

This Temper which I have been describing is almost always complicated with Ideas of the high Prerogatives of human Nature, of a sacred unalienable Birthright, which no Man has conferr'd upon us, and which neither Kings can take, nor Senates give away, which we may justly assert whenever and by whomsoever it is attacked, and which, if ever it should happen to be lost, we may take the first Opportunity to recover.

The natural Consequence of these Chimeras is Contempt of Authority, and an Irreverence for any Superiority but what is founded upon Merit, and their Notions of Merit are very peculiar, for it is among them no great Proof of Merit to be wealthy and powerful, to wear a Garter or a Star, to command a Regiment or a Senate, to have the Ear of the Minister or of the King, or to possess any of those Virtues and Excellencies which among us entitle a Man to little less than Worship and Prostration.

We may therefore easily conceive that Mr *Brooke* thought himself entitled to be importunate for a License, because, in his own Opinion, he deserved one, and to complain thus loudly at the Repulse he met with.

His Complaints will have, I hope, but little Weight

with the Publick, since the Opinions of the Sect in which he is enlisted are exposed and shown to be evidently and demonstrably opposite to that System of Subordination and Dependence to which we are indebted for the present Tranquillity of the Nation, and that Chearfulness and Readiness with which the two Houses concur in all our Designs.

I shall however, to silence him intirely, or at least to shew those of our Party, that he ought to be silent, consider singly every Instance of Hardship and Oppression which he has dared to publish in the Papers, and to publish in such a Manner that I hope no Man will condemn me for Want of Candour in becoming an Advocate for the Ministry, if I can consider his Advertisements as nothing less than AN APPEAL TO HIS COUNTRY.

Let me be forgiven if I cannot speak with Temper of such Insolence as this: Is a Man without Title, Pension, or Place, to suspect the Impartiality or the Judgment of those who are intrusted with the Administration of publick Affairs? Is he, when the Law is not strictly observed in Regard to him, to think himself *aggrieved*, to tell his Sentiments in Print, assert his Claim to better Usage, and fly for Redress to another Tribunal?

If such Practices are permitted, I will not venture to foretell the Effects of them, the Ministry may soon be convinced that such Sufferers will find Compassion, and that it is safer not to bear hard upon them than to allow them to complain.

The Power of Licensing in general, being firmly established by an Act of Parliament, our Poet has not attempted to call in Question, but contents himself with censuring the Manner in which it has been executed, so that I am not now engaged to assert the Licenser's Authority, but to defend his Conduct.

The Poet seems to think himself aggrieved, because the Licenser kept his Tragedy in his Hands one and twenty Days, whereas the Law allows him to detain it only fourteen.

Where will the Insolence of the Malcontents end? Or how are such unreasonable Expectations possibly to be satisfied? Was it ever known that a Man exalted into a high Station dismissed a Suppliant in the Time limited by Law? Ought not Mr *Brooke* to think himself happy that his Play was not detained longer? If he had been kept a Year in Suspense, what Redress could he have obtained? Let the Poets remember when they appear before the Licenser, or his Deputy, that they stand at the Tribunal from which there is no Appeal permitted, and where nothing will so well become them as Reverence and Submission.

Mr *Brooke* mentions in his Preface his Knowledge of the Laws of his own Country; had he extended his Enquiries to the Civil Law, he could have found a full Justification of the Licenser's Conduct, *Boni Judicis est ampliare suam auctoritatem.* [It is the sign of a good judge that he should augment his authority]

If then it be *the Business of a good Judge to enlarge his Authority*, was it not in the Licenser the utmost Clemency and Forbearance, to extend fourteen Days only to twenty-one.

I suppose this great Man's Inclination to perform at least this Duty of a good Judge, is not questioned by any, either of his Friends or Enemies, I may therefore venture to hope that he will extend his Power by proper Degrees, and that I shall live to see a Malecontent Writer earnestly soliciting for the Copy of a Play, which he had delivered to the Licenser twenty Years before.

I waited, says he, *often on the Licenser, and with the utmost Importunity entreated an Answer.* Let Mr *Brooke* consider whether that Importunity was not a sufficient Reason for the Disappointment. Let him reflect how much more decent it had been to have waited the Leisure of a great Man, than to have pressed upon him with repeated Petitions, and to have intruded upon those precious Moments which he has dedicated to the Service of his Country.

Mr *Brooke* was doubtless led into this improper Manner of acting, by an erroneous Notion that the Grant of a License was not an Act of Favour but of Justice, a Mistake into which he could not have fallen, but from a supine Inattention to the Design of the Statute, which was only to bring Poets into Subjection and Dependence, not to encourage good Writers, but to discourage all.

There lies no Obligation upon the Licenser to grant his Sanction to a Play, however excellent, nor can Mr *Brooke* demand any Reparation, whatever Applause his Performance may meet with.

Another Grievance is, that the Licenser assigned no Reason for his Refusal. This is a higher Strain of Insolence than any of the former. Is it for a Poet to demand a Licenser's Reason for his Proceedings? Is he not rather to acquiesce in the Decision of Authority, and conclude that there are Reasons which he cannot comprehend?

Unhappy would it be for Men in Power, were they always obliged to publish the Motives of their Conduct. What is Power but the Liberty of acting without being accountable? The Advocates for the Licensing Act have alledged, that the Lord Chamberlain has always had Authority to prohibit the Representation of a Play for just Reasons. Why then did we call in all our Force to procure an Act of Parliament? Was it to enable him to do what he has always done, to confirm an Authority which no Man attempted to impair, or pretended to dispute; no, certainly: Our Intention was to invest him with new Privileges, and to empower him to do that *without* Reason, which *with* Reason he could do before.

We have found by long Experience, that to lie under a Necessity of assigning Reasons, is very troublesome, and that many an excellent Design has miscarried by the Loss of Time spent unnecessarily in examining Reasons.

Always to call for Reasons, and always to reject them, shews a strange Degree of Perverseness; yet such is the daily Behaviour of our Adversaries, who have never yet been satisfied with any Reasons that have been offered by us.

They have made it their Practice to demand once a Year the Reasons for which we maintain a Standing Army.

One Year we told them that it was necessary, because all the Nations round us were involved in War; this had no Effect upon them, and therefore resolving to do our utmost for their Satisfaction, we told them the next Year that it was necessary because all the Nations round us were at Peace.

This Reason finding no better Reception than the other, we had Recourse to our Apprehensions of an Invasion from the Pretender, of an Insurrection in Favour of *Gin*, and of a general Disaffection among the People.

But as they continue still impenetrable, and oblige us still to assign our annual Reasons, we shall spare no Endeavours to procure such as may be more satisfactory than any of the former.

The Reason we once gave for building Barracks was for Fear of the Plague, and we intend next Year to propose the Augmentation of our Troops for fear of a Famine.

The Committee, by which the Act for Licensing the Stage was drawn up, had too long known the Inconvenience of giving Reasons, and were too well acquainted with the Characters of great Men, to lay the Lord Chamberlain, or his deputy, under any such tormenting Obligation.

Yet lest Mr *Brooke* should imagine that a License was refused him without just Reasons, I shall condescend to treat him with more Regard than he can reasonably expect, and point out such Sentiments as not only justly exposed him to that Refusal, but would have provoked any Ministry less merciful than the present to have inflicted some heavier Penalties upon him.

His Prologue is filled with such Insinuations as no Friend of our excellent Government can read without Indignation and Abhorrence, and cannot but be owned to be a proper Introduction to such Scenes as seem designed to kindle in the Audience a Flame of Opposition, Patriotism, Publick Spirit, and Independency, that Spirit which we have so long endeavoured to suppress,

and which cannot be revived without the entire Subver-
sion of all our Schemes.

This seditious Poet not content with making an open
Attack upon us, by declaring in plain Terms, that he
looks upon Freedom as the only Source of publick Happiness and national Security, has endeavoured with Subtlety, equal to his Malice, to make us suspicious of our
firmest Friends, to infect our Consultations with Distrust,
and to ruin us by disuniting us.

This indeed will not be easily effected, an Union
founded upon Interest and cemented by Dependance is
naturally lasting: But Confederacies which owe their
Rise to Virtue or mere Conformity of Sentiments are
quickly dissolved, since no Individual has any Thing
either to hope or fear for himself, and publick Spirit is
generally too weak to combat with private Passions.

The Poet has, however, attempted to weaken our
Combination by an artful and sly Assertion, which, if
suffered to remain unconfuted, may operate by Degrees
upon our Minds in the Days of Leisure and Retirement
which are now approaching, and perhaps fill us with such
Surmises as may at least very much embarrass our Affairs.

The Law by which the *Swedes* justified their Opposition to the incroachments of the King of *Denmark* he
not only calls

Great Nature's Law, the Law within the Breast

But proceeds to tell us that it is

——*Stamp'd by Heav'n upon th' unletter'd Mind.*

By which he evidently intends to insinuate a Maxim which is, I hope, as false as it is pernicious, that Men are naturally fond of Liberty till those unborn Ideas and Desires are effaced by Literature.

The Author, if he be not a Man mew'd up in his solitary Study and entirely unacquainted with the Conduct of the present Ministry, must know that we have hitherto acted upon different Principles. We have always regarded *Letters* as great Obstructions to our Scheme of Subordination, and have therefore, when we have heard of any Man remarkably *unletter'd*, carefully noted him down as the most proper Person for any Employments of Trust or Honour, and considered him as a Man in whom we could safely repose our most important Secrets.

From among the uneducated and *unletter'd* we have chosen not only our Embassadors and other Negotiators, but even our Journalists and Pamphleteers, nor have we had any Reason to change our Measures or to repent of the Confidence which we have placed in Ignorance.

Are we now therefore to be told that this Law is

Stamp'd upon th' unletter'd Mind?

Are we to suspect our Place-men, our Pensioners, our Generals, our Lawyers, our best Friends in both Houses, all our Adherents among the Atheists and Infidels, and our very Gazetteers, Clerks, and Court-pages, as Friends to Independency? Doubtless this is the Tendency of his Assertion, but we have known them too long to be thus imposed upon, the *unletter'd* have been our warmest and most constant Defenders, nor have we omitted any

Thing to deserve their Favour, but have always endeavoured to raise their Reputation, extend their Influence, and encrease their Number.

In his first Act he abounds with Sentiments very inconsistent with the Ends for which the Power of Licensing was granted; to enumerate them all would be to transcribe a great Part of his Play, a Task which I shall very willingly leave to others, who, tho' true Friends to the Government, are not inflamed with Zeal so fiery and impatient as mine, and therefore do not feel the same Emotions of Rage and Resentment at the Sight of those infamous Passages, in which Venality and Dependence are presented as mean in themselves, and productive of Remorse and Infelicity.

One Line which ought, in my Opinion, to be erased from every Copy by a special Act of Parliament, is mentioned by *Anderson*, as pronounced by the Hero in his Sleep,

O Sweden, *O my Country, yet I'll save thee.*

This Line I have Reason to believe thrown out as a kind of Watch-word for the opposing Faction, who, when they meet in their seditious Assemblies, have been observed to lay their Hands upon their Breasts, and cry out with great Vehemence of Accent.

O B——, *O my Country, yet I'll save thee.*

In the second Scene he endeavours to fix Epithets of Contempt upon those Passions and Desires which have been always found most useful to the Ministry, and most opposite to the Spirit of Independency.

> *Base Fear, the Laziness of Lust, gross Appetites,*
> *These are the Ladders and the grov'ling Foot-stool*
> *From whence the Tyrant rises——*
> *Secure and scepter'd in the Soul's Servility*
> *He has debauched the Genius of our Country*
> *And rides triumphant, while her captive Sons*
> *Await his Nod, the silken Slaves of Pleasure,*
> *Or fettered in their Fears.——*

Thus is that decent Submission to our Superiors, and that proper Awe of Authority which we are taught in Courts, termed *base Fear* and the *Servility of the Soul.* Thus are those Gayeties and Enjoyments, those elegant Amusements, and lulling Pleasures which the Followers of a Court are blessed with, as the just Rewards of their Attendance and Submission, degraded to *Lust, Grossness,* and *Debauchery.* The Author ought to be told, that Courts are not to be mentioned with so little Ceremony, and that though Gallantries and Amours are admitted there, it is almost Treason to suppose them infected with Debauchery or Lust.

It is observable that when this hateful Writer has conceived any Thought of an uncommon Malignity, a Thought which tends in a more particular Manner to excite the Love of Liberty, animate the Heat of Patriotism, or degrade the Majesty of Kings, he takes Care to put it in the Mouth of his Hero, that it may be more forcibly impressed upon his Reader. Thus *Gustavus*, speaking of his Tatters, cries out,

> ——*Yes, my* Arvida,
> *Beyond the Sweeping of the proudest Train*
> *That shades a Monarch's Heel, I prize these Weeds,*
> *For they are sacred to my Country's Freedom.*

Here this abandoned Son of Liberty makes a full Discovery of his execrable Principles, the Tatters of *Gustavus*, the usual Dress of the Assertors of these Doctrines, are of more Divinity, because they are sacred to Freedom than the sumptuous and magnificent Robes of Regality itself. Such Sentiments are truly detestable, nor could any Thing be an Aggravation of the Author's Guilt, except his ludicrous Manner of mentioning a Monarch.

The *Heel of a Monarch*, or even the Print of his *Heel* is a Thing too venerable and sacred to be treated with such Levity, and placed in Contrast with Rags and Poverty. He that will speak contemptuously of the *Heel* of a *Monarch* will, whenever he can with Security, speak contemptuously of his Head.

These are the most glaring Passages which have occurr'd, in the Perusal of the first Pages; my Indignation will not suffer me to proceed farther, and I think much better of the Licenser, than to believe he went so far.

In the few Remarks which I have set down, the Reader will easily observe that I have strained no Expression beyond its natural Import, and have divested myself of all Heat, Partiality, and Prejudice.

So far therefore is Mr *Brooke* from having received any hard or unwarrantable Treatment, that the Licenser has only acted in Pursuance of that Law to which he owes his Power, a Law which every Admirer of the Administration must own to be very necessary, and to have produced very salutary Effects.

I am indeed surprised that this great Office is not drawn out into a longer series of Deputations, since it might afford a gainful and reputable Employment to a great Number of the Friends of the Government; and I should think instead of having immediate Recourse to the Deputy-licenser himself, it might be sufficient Honour for any Poet, except the Laureat, to stand bareheaded in the Presence of the Deputy of the Deputy's Deputy in the nineteenth Subordination.

Such a Number cannot but be thought necessary if we take into Consideration the great Work of drawing up an *Index Expurgatorius* to all the old Plays; which is, I hope, already undertaken, or if it has been hitherto unhappily neglected, I take this Opportunity to recommend.

The Productions of our old Poets are crouded with Passages very unfit for the Ears of an *English* Audience, and which cannot be pronounced without irritating the Minds of the People.

This Censure I do not confine to those Lines in which Liberty, natural Equality, wicked Ministers, deluded Kings, mean Arts of Negotiation, venal Senates, mercenary Troops, oppressive Officers, servile and exorbitant Taxes, universal Corruption, the Luxuries of a Court, the Miseries of the People, the Decline of Trade, or the Happiness of Independency are directly mentioned.

These are such glaring Passages as cannot be suffered to pass without the most supine and criminal Negligence. I hope the Vigilance of the Licensers will extend to all such Speeches and Soliloquies as tend to recommend the Pleasures of Virtue, the Tranquillity of an uncorrupted Head, and the Satisfactions of conscious Innocence; for though such Strokes as these do not appear to a common Eye to threaten any Danger to the Government, yet it is well known to more penetrating Observers that they have such Consequences as cannot be too diligently obviated, or too cautiously avoided.

A Man who becomes once enamour'd of the Charms of Virtue is apt to be very little concerned about the Acquisition of Wealth or Titles, and is therefore not easily induced to act in a Manner contrary to his real Sentiments, or to vote at the Word of Command; by contracting his Desires, and regulating his Appetites, he wants much less than other Men, and every one versed in the Arts of Government can tell, that Men are more easily influenced in Proportion as they are more necessitous.

This is not the only Reason why Virtue should not receive too much Countenance from a licensed Stage; her Admirers and Followers are not only naturally independent, but learn such a uniform and consistent Manner of speaking and acting, that they frequently by the mere Force of artless Honesty surmount all the Obstacles which Subtlety and Politicks can throw in their way, and obtain their Ends in spite of the most profound and sagacious Ministry.

Such then are the Passages to be expunged by the

Licensers: In many Parts indeed the Speeches will be imperfect, and the Action appear not regularly conducted, but the Poet Laureat may easily supply these Vacuities by inserting some of his own Verses in praise of Wealth, Luxury, and Venality.

But alas! all those pernicious Sentiments which we shall banish from the Stage, will be vented from the Press, and more studiously read because they are prohibited.

I cannot but earnestly implore the Friends of the Government to leave no Art untry'd by which we may hope to succeed in our Design of extending the Power of the Licenser to the Press, and of making it criminal to publish any Thing without an *Imprimatur*. ['let it be published'; by extension, the permission to print something]

How much would this single Law lighten the mighty Burden of State Affairs? With how much Security might our Ministers enjoy their Honours, their Places, their Reputations, and their Admirers, could they once suppress those malicious Invectives which are at present so industriously propagated, and so eagerly read, could they hinder any Arguments but their own from coming to the Ears of the People, and stop effectually the Voice of Cavil and Enquiry.

I cannot but indulge myself a little while by dwelling on this pleasing Scene, and imagining those *Halcyon-days* in which no Politicks shall be read but those of the *Gazetteer*, nor any Poetry but that of the Laureat; when we shall hear of nothing but the successful Negotiations of our Ministers, and the great Actions of——.

How much happier would this State be, than those

perpetual Jealousies and Contentions which are insepar-
able from Knowledge and Liberty, and which have for
many Years kept this Nation in perpetual Commotions.

But these are Times rather to be wished for than
expected, for such is the Nature of our unquiet
Countrymen, that if they are not admitted to the Know-
ledge of Affairs, they are always suspecting their
Governors of Designs prejudicial to their Interest; they
have not the least Notion of the pleasing Tranquillity of
Ignorance, nor can be brought to imagine that they are
kept in the Dark, lest too much Light should hurt their
Eyes. They have long claimed a Right of directing their
Superiors, and are exasperated at the least Mention of
Secrets of State.

This Temper makes them very readily encourage any
Writer or Printer, who, at the Hazard of his Life or
Fortune, will give them any Information; and while this
Humour prevails there never will be wanting some
daring Adventurer who will write in Defence of Liberty,
and some zealous or avaricious Printer who will disperse
his Papers.

It has never yet been found that any Power, however
vigilant or despotick, has been able to prevent the Publication of seditious Journals, Ballads, Essays and Dissertations, *Considerations on the present State of Affairs*, and
Enquiries into the Conduct of the Administration.

Yet I must confess, that considering the Success with
which the present Ministry has hitherto proceeded in
their Attempts to drive out of the World the old Prejudices of Patriotism and publick Spirit, I cannot but enter-
tain some Hopes that what has been so often attempted

by their Predecessors, is reserved to be accomplished by their superior Abilities.

If I might presume to advise them upon this great Affair, I should dissuade them from any direct Attempt upon the Liberty of the Press, which is the Darling of the common People, and therefore cannot be attacked without immediate Danger. They may proceed by a more sure and silent Way, and attain the desired End without Noise, Detraction, or Opposition.

There are scatter'd over this Kingdom several little Seminaries in which the lower Ranks of People, and the younger Sons of our Nobility and Gentry are taught, from their earliest infancy, the pernicious Arts of Spelling and Reading, which they afterwards continue to practise very much to the Disturbance of their own Quiet, and the Interruption of ministerial Measures.

These Seminaries may, by an Act of Parliament, be at once suppressed, and that our Posterity be deprived of all Means of reviving this corrupt Method of Education, it may be made Felony to teach to read, without a License from the Lord Chamberlain.

This Expedient, which I hope will be carefully concealed from the Vulgar, must infallibly answer the great End proposed by it, and set the Power of the Court not only above the Insults of the Poets, but in a short Time above the Necessity of providing against them. The Licenser having his Authority thus extended will in Time enjoy the Title and the Salary without the Trouble of exercising his Power, and the Nation will rest at length in Ignorance and Peace.

An Essay *on* EPITAPHS

Tho' Criticism has been cultivated in every Age of Learning, by Men of great Abilities and extensive Knowledge, till the Rules of Writing are become rather burdensome than instructive to the Mind; tho' almost every Species of Composition has been the Subject of particular Treatises, and given Birth to Definitions, Distinctions, Precepts and Illustrations; yet no Critic of Note, that has fallen within my Observation, has hitherto thought *Sepulchral Inscriptions* worthy of a minute Examination, or pointed out with proper Accuracy their Beauties and Defects.

The Reasons of this Neglect it is useless to enquire, and perhaps impossible to discover; it might be justly expected that this Kind of Writing would have been the favourite Topic of Criticism, and that Self-Love might have produced some Regard for it, in those Authors that have crowded Libraries with elaborate Dissertations upon *Homer*; since to afford a Subject for heroick Poems is the Privilege of very few, but every Man may expect to be recorded in an Epitaph, and, therefore, finds some Interest in providing that his Memory may not suffer by an unskilful Panegyrick.

If our Prejudices in favour of Antiquity deserve to have any Part in the Regulation of our Studies, EPITAPHS seem entitled to more than common Regard, as they are probably of the same Age with the Art of Writing. The most ancient Structures in the World, the Pyramids, are supposed to be Sepulchral Monuments, which either Pride or Gratitude erected, and the same Passions which incited Men to such laborious and expensive Methods of preserving their own Memory, or that of their Benefactors, would doubtless incline them not to neglect any easier Means by which ye same Ends might be obtained. Nature and Reason have dictated to every Nation, that to preserve good Actions from Oblivion, is both the Interest and Duty of Mankind; and therefore we find no People acquainted with the Use of Letters that omitted to grace the Tombs of their Heroes and wise Men with panegyrical Inscriptions.

To examine, therefore, in what the Perfection of EPITAPHS consists, and what Rules are to be observed in composing them, will be at least of as much use as other critical Enquiries; and for assigning a few Hours to such Disquisitions, great Examples at least, if not strong Reasons, may be pleaded.

An EPITAPH, as the word itself implies, is an *Inscription on a Tomb*, and in its most extensive Import may admit indiscriminately Satire or Praise. But as Malice has seldom produced Monuments of Defamation, and the Tombs hitherto raised have been the Work of Friendship and Benevolence, Custom has contracted the Original Latitude of the *Word*, so that it signifies in the general Acceptation an *Inscription engraven on a Tomb in Honour of the Person deceased*.

As Honours are paid to the Dead in order to incite others to the Imitation of their Excellencies, the principal Intention of EPITAPHS is to perpetuate the examples of

Virtue, that the Tomb of a good Man may supply the Want of his Presence, and Veneration for his Memory produce the same Effect as the Observation of his Life. Those EPITAPHS are, therefore, the most perfect, which set Virtue in the strongest Light, and are best adapted to exalt the Reader's Ideas, and rouse his Emulation.

To this End it is not always necessary to recount the Actions of a Hero, or enumerate the Writings of a Philosopher; to imagine such Informations necessary, is to detract from their Characters, or to suppose their Works mortal, or their Atchievements in danger of being forgotten. The bare Name of such Men answers every Purpose of a long Inscription.

Had only the Name of Sir ISAAC NEWTON been subjoined to the Design upon his Monument, instead of a long Detail of his Discoveries, which no Philosopher can want, and which none but a Philosopher can understand, those by whose Direction it was raised, had done more Honour both to him and to themselves.

This indeed is a Commendation which it requires no Genius to bestow, but which can never become vulgar or contemptible, if bestow'd with Judgment; because no single Age produces many Men of Merit superior to Panegyrick. None but the first Names can stand unassisted against the Attacks of Time, and if Men raised to Reputation by Accident or Caprice have nothing but their Names engraved on their Tombs, there is Danger lest in a few Years the Inscription require an Interpreter. Thus have their Expectations been disappointed who honoured *Picus* of *Mirandola*, with this pompous Epitaph,

Hic situs est PICUS MIRANDOLA, *cætera norunt*
  Et Tagus *et* Ganges, *forsan et* Antipodes.
['Here lies Pico della Mirandola: the Tagus, the Ganges, even the Antipodes, know the rest.']

His Name then celebrated in the remotest Corners of the Earth is now almost forgotten, and his Works, then studied, admired, and applauded, are now mouldering in Obscurity.

Next in Dignity to the bare Name is a short Character simple and unadorned, without Exaggeration, Superlatives, or Rhetoric. Such were the Inscriptions in Use among the *Romans*, in which the Victories gained by their Emperors were commemorated by a single Epithet; as Cæsar *Germanicus*, Cæsar *Dacicus*, *Germanicus*, *Illyricus*. Such would be this Epitaph, ISAACUS NEWTONUS, *Naturæ Legibus investigatis, hic quiescit.* ['Having searched out the laws of nature, Isaac Newton rests here.']

But to far the greatest Part of Mankind a longer Encomium is necessary for the Publication of their Virtues, and the Preservation of their Memories, and in the Composition of these it is that Art is principally required, and Precepts therefore may be useful.

In writing EPITAPHS, one circumstance is to be considered, which affects no other Composition; the Place in which they are now commonly found restrains them to a particular Air of Solemnity, and debars them from the Admission of all lighter or gayer Ornaments. In this it is that the Stile of an EPITAPH necessarily differs from that of an ELEGY. The Customs of burying our Dead either in or near our Churches, perhaps originally founded on a rational Design of fitting the Mind for religious Exercises, by laying before it the most affecting Proofs of the Uncertainty of Life, makes it proper to exclude from our EPITAPHS all such Allusions as are contrary to the Doctrines for the Propagation of which the Churches are erected, and to the End for which those who peruse the Monuments must be supposed to come thither. Nothing is, therefore, more ridiculous than to copy the *Roman* Inscriptions which were engraven on Stones by the Highway, and composed by those who generally reflected on Mortality only to excite in themselves and others a quicker Relish of Pleasure, and a more luxurious Enjoyment of Life, and whose Regard for the Dead extended no farther than a Wish that *the Earth might be light upon them*.

All Allusions to the Heathen Mythology are therefore absurd, and all Regard for the senseless Remains of a dead Man impertinent and superstitious. One of the first Distinctions of the primitive Christians was their Neglect of bestowing Garlands on the Dead, in which they are very rationally defended by their Apologist in *Minutius Felix. We lavish no Flowers nor Odours on the Dead*, says he, *because they have no Sense of Fragrance or of Beauty*. We profess to Reverence the Dead not for their Sake but for our own. It is therefore always with Indignation or Contempt that I read the Epitaph on *Cowley*, a Man whose Learning and Poetry were his lowest Merits.

> *Aurea dum late volitant tua Scripta per Orbem,*
> *Et fama eternum vivis, divine Poeta,*

Hic placida jaceas requie, custodiat urnam
Cana, Fides, vigilentque perenni Lampade Musæ!
Sit sacer ille locus, nec quis temerarius ausit
Sacrilega turbare manu venerabile bustum,
Intacti maneant, maneant per sæcula dulces
COWLEII *cineres, serventq; immobile Saxum.*

['O divine poet, while your golden writings fly far and wide throughout the globe and you live perpetually in fame, may you lie here in peaceful rest. May aged faith guard your urn, and may the muses keep watch over you with their inextinguishable torch. May this place be sacred, and let no one be so rash as to dare disturb this venerable bust with sacrilegious hand. May Cowley's dust rest undisturbed, rest through sweet ages, and may his tombstone be unmoved.']

To pray, that ye Ashes of a Friend may lie undisturbed, and that the Divinities that favoured him in his Life, may watch for ever round him to preserve his Tomb from Violation and drive Sacrilege away, is only rational in him who believes the Soul interested in the Repose of the Body, and the Powers which he invokes for its Protection able to preserve it. To censure such Expressions as contrary to Religion, or as Remains of Heathen Superstition, would be too great a Degree of Severity. I condemn them only as uninstructive and unaffecting, as too ludicrous for Reverence or Grief, for Christianity and a Temple.

That the Designs and Decorations of Monuments, ought likewise to be formed with the same Regard to the Solemnity of the Place, cannot be denied; It is an established Principle that all Ornaments owe their Beauty to their Propriety. The same Glitter of Dress that adds Graces to Gayety and Youth, would make Age and Dignity contemptible. CHARON with his Boat is far from heightening the awful Grandeur of the universal Judgment, tho' drawn by *Angelo* himself; nor is it easy to imagine a greater Absurdity than that of gracing the Walls of a Christian Temple with the Figure of *Mars* leading a Hero to Battle, or *Cupids* sporting round a Virgin. The Pope who defaced the Statues of the Deities, at the Tomb of *Sannazarius* is, in my opinion, more easily to be defended than he that erected them.

It is for the same Reason improper to address the EPITAPH to the Passenger, a Custom which in injudicious Veneration for Antiquity introduced again at the Revival of Letters, and which, among many others, *Passeratius* suffered to mislead him in his EPITAPH upon the Heart of *Henry* King of *France*, who was stabbed by *Clement* the Monk, which yet deserves to be inserted, for the Sake of showing how beautiful even Improprieties may become in the Hands of a good Writer.

> *Adsta, Viator, et dole regum vices.*
> *Cor Regis isto conditur sub marmore,*
> *Qui jura Gallis, jura Sarmatis dedit;*
> *Tectus Cucullo hunc sustulit Sicarius.*
> Abi, Viator, et dole regum vices.

['Pause, traveller, and commiserate the fate of kings. Beneath this marble is laid the heart of a king who gave laws equally to the French and to the Poles. A murderer hidden beneath a cowl killed him. Pass on, traveller, and commiserate the fate of kings.']

In the Monkish Ages, however ignorant and unpolished, the EPITAPHS were drawn up with far greater Propriety than can be shown in those, which more enlightened Times have produced.

> *Orate pro Anima* —— *miserrimi Peccatoris*
> ['Pray for the soul of —— a most miserable sinner']

was an Address to the last Degree striking and solemn, as it flowed naturally from the Religion then believed, and awakened in the Reader Sentiments of Benevolence for the Deceased, and of Concern for his own Happiness. There was Nothing trifling or ludicrous, Nothing that did not tend to the noblest End, the Propagation of Piety and the Increase of Devotion.

It may seem very superfluous to lay it down as the first Rule for writing EPITAPHS, that the Name of the Deceased is not to be omitted; nor should I have thought such a Precept necessary, had not the Practice of the greatest Writers shewn, that it has not been sufficiently regarded. In most of the Poetical EPITAPHS, the Names for whom they were composed may be sought to no Purpose, being only prefixed on the Monument. To expose yᵉ Absurdity of this Omission, it is only necessary to ask how the EPITAPHS, which have outlived the Stones on which they were inscribed, would have contributed to the Information of Posterity, had they wanted the Names of those whom they celebrated.

In drawing the Character of the Deceased, there are no Rules to be observ'd which do not equally relate to other Compositions. The Praise ought not to be general, because the Mind is lost in the Extent of any indefinite Idea, and cannot be affected with what it cannot comprehend. When we hear only of a good or great Man, we know not in what Class to place him, nor have any Notion of his Character, distinct from that of a thousand others; his Example can have no Effect upon our Conduct, as we have nothing remarkable or eminent to propose to our Imitation. The EPITAPH composed by *Ennius* for his own Tomb, has both the Faults last mentioned,

> *Nemo me decoret lacrumis, nec funera, fletu*
> *Faxit. Cur? – volito vivu' per ora virum.*

[Let no one honour me with tears, nor lay me in the earth with weeping. Why? I live in the mouths of men.]

The Reader of this EPITAPH receives scarce any Idea from it; he neither conceives any Veneration for the Man to whom it belongs, nor is instructed by what Methods this boasted Reputation is to be obtained.

Tho' a sepulchral Inscription is professedly a Panegyric, and, therefore, not confined to historical Impartiality, yet it ought always to be written with regard to Truth. No Man ought to be commended for Virtues which he never possessed, but whoever is curious to know his Faults must enquire after them in other Places; the Monuments of the Dead are not intended to perpetuate the Memory of Crimes, but to exhibit Patterns of

Virtue. On the Tomb of *Mæcenas*, his Luxury is not to be mentioned with his Munificence, nor is the Proscription to find a Place on the Monument of *Augustus*.

The best Subject for EPITAPHS is private Virtue; Virtue exerted in the same Circumstances in which the Bulk of Mankind are placed, and which, therefore, may admit of many Imitators. He that has delivered his Country from Oppression, or freed the World from Ignorance and Error, can excite the Emulation of a very small Number; but he that has repelled the Temptations of Poverty, and disdained to free himself from Distress at the Expence of his Virtue, may animate Multitudes, by his Example, to the same Firmness of Heart and Steadiness of Resolution.

Of this Kind I cannot forbear the Mention of two *Greek* Inscriptions; one upon a Man whose Writings are well known, the other upon a Person whose Memory is preserved only in her EPITAPH, who both lived in Slavery, the most calamitous Estate in human Life.

Ζωσιμη ἡ πριν ἐουσα μονω τω Σωματι δουλη,
    Και τω σωματι νυν εὐρεν ἐλευθεριην.

Zosima, *quæ solo fuit olim Corpore Serva,*
    Corpore nunc etiam libera facta fuit.

Zosima, *who in her Life could only have her Body enslaved,*
    now finds her Body likewise set at Liberty.

It is impossible to read this EPITAPH without being animated to bear the Evils of Life with Constancy, and to support the Dignity of Human Nature under the most pressing Afflictions, both by the Example of the Heroine, whose Grave we behold, and the Prospect of that State in which, to use the Language of the inspired Writers, *The Poor cease from their Labours, and the Weary be at rest.*

The other is upon *Epictetus*, the Stoic Philosopher.

Δουλος Ἐπιχτητος γενομην, χαι Σωμ' ἀναπηρος,
   Και πενιην Ἰρος, χαι Φιλος Ἀθανατοις.

Servus Epictetus, mutilatus corpore, vixi
   Pauperieque Irus, Curaque prima Deum.

Epictetus, *who lies here, was a Slave and a Cripple, poor as
   the Begger in the Proverb, and the Favourite of Heaven.*

In this Distich is comprised the noblest Panegyric, and the most important Instruction. We may learn from it that Virtue is impracticable in no Condition, since *Epictetus* could recommend himself to the Regard of Heaven, amidst the Temptations of Poverty and Slavery; Slavery, which has always been found so destructive to Virtue that in many Languages a Slave and a Thief are expressed by the same Word. And we may be likewise admonished by it, not to lay any Stress on a Man's outward Circumstances in making an Estimate of his real value, since *Epictetus* the Begger, the Cripple, and the Slave, was the Favourite of Heaven.

The Vision of Theodore, the Hermit of Teneriffe, found in his cell

Son of Perseverance, whoever thou art, whose curiosity has led thee hither, read and be wise. He that now calls upon thee is Theodore, the Hermit of Teneriffe, who in the fifty-seventh year of his retreat left this instruction to mankind, lest his solitary hours should be spent in vain.

I was once what thou art now, a groveller on the earth, and a gazer at the sky; I trafficked and heaped wealth together, I loved and was favoured, I wore the robe of honour and heard the music of adulation; I was ambitious, and rose to greatness; I was unhappy, and retired. I sought for some time what I at length found here, a place where all real wants might be easily supplied, and where I might not be under the necessity of purchasing the assistance of men by the toleration of their follies. Here I saw fruits and herbs and water, and here determined to wait the hand of death, which I hope, when at last it comes, will fall lightly upon me.

Forty-eight years had I now passed in forgetfulness of all mortal cares, and without any inclination to wander farther than the necessity of procuring sustenance required; but as I stood one day beholding the rock that overhangs my cell, I found in myself a desire to climb it; and when I was on its top, was in the same manner determined to scale the next, till by degrees I conceived a wish to view the summit of the mountain, at the foot of which I had so long resided. This motion of my thoughts I endeavoured to suppress, not because it appeared criminal, but because it was new; and all change not evidently for the better alarms a mind taught by experience to distrust itself. I was often afraid that my heart was deceiving me, that my impatience of confinement arose from some earthly passion, and that my ardour to survey the works of nature was only a hidden longing to mingle once again in the scenes of life. I therefore endeavoured to settle my thoughts into their former state, but found their distraction every day greater. I was always reproaching myself with the want of happiness within my reach, and at last began to question whether it was not laziness rather than caution that restrained me from climbing to the summit of Teneriffe.

I rose therefore before the day, and began my journey up the steep of the mountain; but I had not advanced far, old as I was and burdened with provisions, when the day began to shine upon me; the declivities grew more precipitous, and the sand slided from beneath my feet; at last, fainting with labour, I arrived at a small plain almost inclosed by rocks, and open only to the east. I sat down to rest awhile, in full persuasion that when I had recovered my strength I should proceed on my design; but when once I had tasted ease, I found many reasons against disturbing it. The branches spread a shade over my head, and the gales of spring wafted odours to my bosom.

As I sat thus, forming alternately excuses for delay,

and resolutions to go forward, an irresistible heaviness suddenly surprised me; I laid my head upon the bank, and resigned myself to sleep: when methought I heard the sound as of the flight of eagles, and a being of more than human dignity stood before me. While I was deliberating how to address him, he took me by the hand with an air of kindness, and asked me solemnly but without severity, 'Theodore, whither art thou going?'

'I am climbing,' answered I, 'to the top of the mountain, to enjoy a more extensive prospect of the works of nature'. 'Attend first', said he, 'to the prospect which this place affords, and what thou dost not understand I will explain. I am one of the benevolent beings who watch over the children of the dust, to preserve them from those evils which will not ultimately terminate in good, and which they do not, by their own faults, bring upon themselves. Look round therefore without fear: observe, contemplate, and be instructed.'

Encouraged by this assurance, I looked and beheld a mountain higher than Teneriffe, to the summit of which the human eye could never reach; when I had tired myself with gazing upon its height, I turned my eyes towards its foot, which I could easily discover, but was amazed to find it without foundation, and placed inconceivably in emptiness and darkness. Thus I stood terrified and confused; above were tracks inscrutable, and below was total vacuity. But my protector, with a voice of admonition, cried out, 'Theodore, be not affrighted, but raise thy eyes again; the Mountain of Existence is before thee, survey it and be wise.'

I then looked with more deliberate attention, and

observed the bottom of the mountain to be of gentle rise, and overspread with flowers; the middle to be more steep, embarrassed with crags, and interrupted by precipices, over which hung branches loaded with fruits, and among which were scattered palaces and bowers. The tracts which my eye could reach nearest the top were generally barren; but there were among the clefts of the rocks a few hardy ever-greens, which, though they did not give much pleasure to the sight or smell, yet seemed to cheer the labour and facilitate the steps of those who were clambering among them.

Then, beginning to examine more minutely the different parts, I observed at a great distance a multitude of both sexes issuing into view from the bottom of the mountain. Their first actions I could not accurately discern; but, as they every moment approached nearer, I found that they amused themselves with gathering flowers under the superintendence of a modest virgin in a white robe, who seemed not over-solicitous to confine them to any settled pace or certain track; for she knew that the whole ground was smooth and solid, and that they could not easily be hurt or bewildered. When, as it often happened, they plucked a thistle for a flower, Innocence, so was she called, would smile at the mistake. 'Happy', said I, 'are they who are under so gentle a government, and yet are safe.' But I had no opportunity to dwell long on the consideration of their felicity; for I found that Innocence continued her attendance but a little way, and seemed to consider only the flowery bottom of the mountain as her proper province. Those whom she abandoned scarcely knew that they were left, before they perceived themselves in the hands of Education, a nymph more severe in her aspect and imperious in her commands, who confined them to certain paths, in their opinion too narrow and too rough. These they were continually solicited to leave, by Appetite, whom Education could never fright away, though she sometimes awed her to such timidity that the effects of her presence were scarcely perceptible. Some went back to the first part of the mountain, and seemed desirous of continuing busied in plucking flowers, but were no longer guarded by Innocence; and such as Education could not force back proceeded up the mountain by some miry road, in which they were seldom seen, and scarcely ever regarded.

As Education led her troop up the mountain, nothing was more observable than that she was frequently giving them cautions to beware of Habits; and was calling out to one or another at every step that a Habit was ensnaring them; that they would be under the dominion of Habit before they perceived their danger; and that those whom Habit should once subdue had little hope of regaining their liberty.

Of this caution, so frequently repeated, I was very solicitous to know the reason, when my protector directed my regard to a troop of pygmies, which appeared to walk silently before those that were climbing the mountain, and each to smooth the way before her follower. I found that I had missed the notice of them before, both because they were so minute as not easily to be discerned, and because they grew every moment nearer in their colour to the objects with which they were surrounded. As the followers of Education did not appear to be sensible of the presence of these dangerous associates, or, ridiculing their diminutive size, did not think it possible that human beings should ever be brought into subjection by such feeble enemies, they generally heard her precepts of vigilance with wonder: and, when they thought her eye withdrawn, treated them with contempt. Nor could I myself think her cautions so necessary as her frequent inculcations seemed to suppose, till I observed that each of these petty beings held secretly a chain in her hand, with which she prepared to bind those whom she found within her power. Yet these Habits under the eye of Education went quietly forward, and seemed very little to increase in bulk or strength; for though they were always willing to join with Appetite, yet when Education kept them apart from her, they would very punctually obey command, and make the narrow roads in which they were confined easier and smoother.

It was observable that their stature was never at a stand, but continually growing or decreasing, yet not always in the same proportions: not could I forbear to express my admiration, when I saw in how much less time they generally gained than lost bulk. Though they grew slowly in the road of Education, it might however be perceived that they grew; but if they once deviated at the call of Appetite, their stature soon became gigantic; and their strength was such that Education pointed out to her tribe many that were led in chains by them, whom she could never more rescue from their slavery. She pointed them out, but with little effect; for all her pupils appeared confident of their own superiority to the strongest Habit, and some seemed in secret to regret that they were hindered from following the triumph of Appetite.

It was the peculiar artifice of Habit not to suffer her power to be felt at first. Those whom she led, she had the address of appearing only to attend, but was continually doubling her chains upon her companions; which were so slender in themselves, and so silently fastened, that while the attention was engaged by other objects, they were not easily perceived. Each link grew tighter as it had been longer worn; and when by continual additions they became so heavy as to be felt, they were very frequently too strong to be broken.

When Education had proceeded in this manner to the part of the mountain where the declivity began to grow craggy, she resigned her charge to two powers of superior aspect. The meaner of them appeared capable of presiding in senates, or governing nations, and yet watched the steps of the other with the most anxious attention, and was visibly confounded and perplexed if ever she suffered her regard to be drawn away. The other seemed to approve her submission as pleasing, but with such a condescension as plainly showed that she claimed it as due; and indeed so great was her dignity and sweetness, that he who would not reverence, must not behold her.

'Theodore,' said my protector, 'be fearless, and be wise; approach these powers, whose dominion extends to all the remaining part of the Mountain of Existence.' I trembled, and ventured to address the inferior nymph, whose eyes, though piercing and awful, I was not able to sustain. 'Bright Power,' said I, 'by whatever name it is lawful to address thee, tell me, thou who presidest here, on what condition thy protection will be granted?' 'It will be granted,' said she, 'only to obedience. I am Reason, of all subordinate beings the noblest and the greatest; who, if thou wilt receive my laws, will reward thee like the rest of my votaries, by conducting thee to Religion.'

Charmed by her voice and aspect, I professed my readiness to follow her. She then presented me to her mistress, who looked upon me with tenderness. I bowed before her, and she smiled.

When Education delivered up those for whose happiness she had been so long solicitous, she seemed to expect that they should express some gratitude for her care, or some regret at the loss of that protection which she had hitherto afforded them. But it was easy to discover, by the alacrity which broke out at her departure, that her presence had been long displeasing, and that she had been teaching those who felt in themselves no want of instruction. They all agreed in rejoicing that they should no longer be subject to her caprices, or disturbed by her dictates, but should be now under the direction only of Reason, to whom they made no doubt of being able to recommend themselves by a steady adherence to all her precepts. Reason counselled them, at their first entrance upon her province, to enlist themselves among the votaries of Religion; and informed them that if they trusted to her alone, they would find the same fate with her other admirers, whom she had not been able to secure against Appetites and Passions, and who, having been seized by Habits in the regions of Desire, had been dragged away to the caverns of Despair. Her admonition was vain, the greater number declared against any other direction, and doubted not but by her superintendency they should climb with safety up the Mountain of Existence. 'My power,' said Reason, 'is to advise, not to compel; I have already told you the danger of your choice. The path seems now plain and even, but there are asperities and pitfalls, over which Religion only can conduct you. Look upwards, and you perceive a mist before you settled upon the highest visible part of the mountain; a mist by which my prospect is terminated, and which is pierced only by the eyes of Religion. Beyond it are the temples of Happiness, in which those who climb the precipice by her direction, after the toil of their pilgrimage, repose for ever. I know not the way, and therefore can only conduct you to a better guide. Pride has sometimes reproached me with the narrowness of my view, but, when she endeavoured to extend it, could only show me, below the mist, the bowers of Content; even they vanished as I fixed my eyes upon them; and those whom she persuaded to travel towards them were enchained by Habits and engulfed by Despair, a cruel tyrant, whose caverns are beyond the darkness on the right side and on the left, from whose prisons none can escape, and whom I cannot teach you to avoid.'

Such was the declaration of Reason to those who demanded her protection. Some that recollected the dictates of Education, finding them now seconded by another authority, submitted with reluctance to the strict decree, and engaged themselves among the followers of Religion, who were distinguished by the uniformity of their march, though many of them were women, and by their continual endeavours to move upwards without appearing to regard the prospects which at every step courted their attention.

All those who determined to follow either Reason or Religion were continually importuned to forsake the road, sometimes by Passions, and sometimes by Appetites, of whom both had reason to boast the success of their artifices; for so many were drawn into by-paths that any way was more populous than the right. The attacks of the Appetites were more impetuous, those of the Passions longer continued. The Appetites turned their followers directly from the true way, but the Passions marched at first in a path nearly in the same direction with that of Reason and Religion; but deviated by slow degrees, till at last they entirely changed their course. Appetite drew aside the dull, and Passion the sprightly. Of the Appetites, Lust was the strongest; and of the Passions, Vanity. The most powerful assault was to be feared when a Passion and an Appetite joined their enticements; and the path of Reason was best followed when a Passion called to one side, and an Appetite to the other.

These seducers had the greatest success upon the followers of Reason, over whom they scarcely ever failed to prevail, except when they counteracted one another. They had not the same triumphs over the votaries of Religion; for though they were often led aside for a time, Religion commonly recalled them by her emissary

Conscience, before Habit had time to enchain them. But they that professed to obey Reason, if once they forsook her, seldom returned; for she had no messenger to summon them but Pride, who generally betrayed her confidence, and employed all her skill to support Passion; and if ever she did her duty, was found unable to prevail, if Habit had interposed.

I soon found that the great danger to the followers of Religion was only from Habit; every other power was easily resisted, nor did they find any difficulty, when they inadvertently quitted her, to find her again by the direction of Conscience, unless they had given time to Habit to draw her chain behind them, and bar up the way by which they had wandered. Of some of those, the condition was justly to be pitied, who turned at every call of Conscience, and tried, but without effect, to burst the chains of Habit: saw Religion walking forward at a distance, saw her with reverence, and longed to join her; but were, whenever they approached her, withheld by Habit, and languished in sordid bondage, which they could not escape, though they scorned and hated it.

It was evident that the Habits were so far from growing weaker by these repeated contests that if they were not totally overcome, every struggle enlarged their bulk and increased their strength; and a Habit opposed and victorious was more than twice as strong as before the contest. The manner in which those who were weary of their tyranny endeavoured to escape from them appeared by the event to be generally wrong; they tried to loose their chains one by one, and to retreat by the same degrees as they advanced; but before the deliverance was completed, Habit always threw new chains upon her fugitive; nor did any escape her but those who, by an effort sudden and violent, burst their shackles at once, and left her at a distance; and even of these, many, rushing too precipitately forward, and hindered by their terrors from stopping where they were safe, were fatigued with their own vehemence, and resigned themselves again to that power from whom an escape must be so dearly bought, and whose tyranny was little felt, except when it was resisted.

Some however there always were, who, when they found Habit prevailing over them, called upon Reason or Religion for assistance; each of them willingly came to the succour of her suppliant, but neither with the same strength, nor the same success. Habit, insolent with her power, would often presume to parley with Reason, and offer to loose some of her chains if the rest might remain. To this Reason, who was never certain of victory, frequently consented, but always found her concession destructive, and saw the captive led away by Habit to his former slavery. Religion never submitted to treaty, but held out her hand with certainty of conquest; and if the captive to whom she gave it did not quit his hold, always led him away in triumph, and placed him in the direct path to the Temple of Happiness, where Reason never failed to congratulate his deliverance, and encourage his adherence to that power to whose timely succour he was indebted for it.

When the traveller was again placed in the road of Happiness, I saw Habit again gliding before him, but reduced to the stature of a dwarf, without strength and without activity; but when the Passions or Appetites which had before seduced him made their approach, Habit would on a sudden start into size, and with unexpected violence push him towards them. The wretch, thus impelled on one side, and allured on the other, too frequently quitted the road of Happiness, to which, after his second deviation from it, he rarely returned. But, by a timely call upon Religion, the force of Habit was eluded, her attacks grew fainter, and at last her correspondence with the enemy was entirely destroyed. She then began to employ those restless faculties in compliance with the power which she could not overcome; and as she grew again in stature and in strength, cleared away the asperities of the road to Happiness.

From this road I could not easily withdraw my attention, because all who travelled it appeared cheerful and satisfied; and the farther they proceeded, the greater appeared their alacrity, and the stronger their conviction of the wisdom of their guide. Some who had never deviated but by short excursions had Habit in the middle of their passage vigorously supporting them, and driving off their Appetites and Passions which attempted to interrupt their progress. Others, who had entered this road late, or had long forsaken it, were toiling on without her help at least, and commonly against her endeavours. But I observed, when they approached to the barren top, that few were able to proceed without some support from Habit; and that they whose Habits were strong advanced towards the mists with little emotion, and entered them at last with calmness and confidence; after which, they were seen only by the eye of Religion; and though Reason looked after them with the most earnest curiosity, she could only obtain a faint glimpse, when her mistress, to enlarge her prospect, raised her from the ground. Reason, however, discerned that they were safe, but Religion saw that they were happy.

'Now, Theodore,' said my Protector, 'withdraw thy view from the regions of obscurity, and see the fate of those who, when they were dismissed by Education, would admit no direction but that of Reason. Survey their wanderings, and be wise.'

I looked then upon the road of Reason, which was indeed, so far as it reached, the same with that of Religion, nor had Reason discovered it but by her instruction. Yet when she had once been taught it, she clearly saw that it was right; and Pride had sometimes incited her to declare that she discovered it herself, and persuaded her to offer herself as a guide to Religion; whom after many vain experiments she found it her highest privilege to follow. Reason was however at last well instructed in part of the way, and appeared to teach it with some success, when her precepts were not misrepresented by Passion, or her influence overborne by Appetite. But neither of these enemies was she able to resist. When Passion seized upon her votaries, she seldom attempted opposition: she seemed indeed to contend with more vigour against Appetite, but was generally overwearied in the contest; and if either of her opponents had confederated with Habit, her authority was wholly at an end. When Habit endeavoured to captivate the votaries of Religion, she grew by slow degrees, and gave time to escape; but in seizing the unhappy followers of Reason, she proceeded as one that had nothing to fear, and enlarged her size, and doubled her chains without intermission, and without reserve.

Of those who forsook the directions of Reason, some were led aside by the whispers of Ambition, who was perpetually pointing to stately palaces, situated on eminences on either side, recounting the delights of affluence, and boasting the security of power. They were easily persuaded to follow her, and Habit quickly threw her chains upon them; they were soon convinced of the folly of their choice, but few of them attempted to return. Ambition led them forward from precipice to precipice, where many fell and were seen no more. Those that escaped were, after a long series of hazards, generally delivered over to Avarice, and enlisted by her in the service of Tyranny, where they continued to heap up gold till their patrons or their heirs pushed them headlong at last into the caverns of Despair.

Others were enticed by Intemperance to ramble in search of those fruits that hung over the rocks, and filled the air with their fragrance. I observed that the Habits which hovered about these soon grew to an enormous size, nor were there any who less attempted to return to Reason, or sooner sunk into the gulfs that lay before them. When these first quitted the road, Reason looked after them with a frown of contempt, but had little expectations of being able to reclaim them; for the bowl of intoxication was of such qualities as to make them lose all regard but for the present moment; neither Hope nor Fear could enter their retreats; and Habit had so absolute a power that even Conscience, if Religion had employed her in their favour, would not have been able to force an entrance.

There were others whose crime it was rather to neglect Reason than to disobey her; and who retreated from the heat and tumult of the way, not to the bowers of Intemperance, but to the maze of Indolence. They had this peculiarity in their condition, that they were always in sight of the road of Reason, always wishing for her presence, and always resolving to return tomorrow. In these was most eminently conspicuous the subtlety of Habit, who hung imperceptible shackles upon them, and was every moment leading them farther from the road, which they always imagined that they had the power of reaching. They wandered on from one double of the labyrinth to another with the chains of Habit hanging secretly upon them, till, as they advanced, the flowers grew paler, and the scents fainter; they proceeded in their dreary march without pleasure in their progress, yet without power to return; and had this aggravation above all others, that they were criminal but not delighted. The drunkard for a time laughed over his wine; the ambitious man triumphed in the miscarriage of his rival; but the captives of Indolence had neither superiority nor merriment. Discontent lowered in their looks, and Sadness hovered round their shades; yet they crawled on reluctant and gloomy, till they arrived at the depth of the recess, varied only with poppies and nightshade, where the dominion of Indolence terminates, and the hopeless wanderer is delivered up to Melancholy: the chains of Habit are riveted for ever; and

Melancholy, having tortured her prisoner for a time, consigns him at last to the cruelty of Despair.

While I was musing on this miserable scene, my Protector called out to me, 'Remember, Theodore, and be wise, and let not Habit prevail against thee.' I started, and beheld myself surrounded by the rocks of Teneriffe; the birds of light were singing in the trees, and the glances of the morning darted upon me.

On Theory and Practice

——————————————— *Nil fuit unquam*

Sic dispar sibi ———————————————

HOR.

Sure such a various creature ne'er was known.

FRANCIS.

Among the many inconsistencies which folly produces, or infirmity suffers in the human mind, there has often been observed a manifest and striking contrariety between the life of an author and his writings; and Milton, in a letter to a learned stranger, by whom he had been visited, with great reason congratulates himself upon the consciousness of being found equal to his own character, and having preserved in a private and familiar interview that reputation which his works had procured him.

Those whom the appearance of virtue, or the evidence of genius, have tempted to a nearer knowledge of the writer in whose performances they may be found, have indeed had frequent reason to repent their curiosity; the bubble that sparkled before them has become common water at the touch; the phantom of perfection has vanished when they wished to press it to their bosom. They have lost the pleasure of imagining how far humanity may be exalted, and, perhaps, felt themselves less inclined to toil up the steeps of virtue, when they observe those who seem best able to point the way, loitering below, as either afraid of the labour, or doubtful of the reward.

It has been long the custom of the oriental monarchs to hide themselves in gardens and palaces, to avoid the conversation of mankind, and to be known to their subjects only by their edicts. The same policy is no less necessary to him that writes, than to him that governs; for men would not more patiently submit to be taught, than commanded, by one known to have the same follies and weaknesses with themselves. A sudden intruder into the closet of an author would perhaps feel equal indignation with the officer, who having long solicited admission into the presence of Sardanapalus, saw him not consulting upon laws, enquiring into grievances, or modelling armies, but employed in feminine amusements, and directing the ladies in their work.

It is not difficult to conceive, however, that for many reasons a man writes much better than he lives. For, without entering into refined speculations, it may be shown much easier to design than to perform. A man proposes his schemes of life in a state of abstraction and disengagement, exempt from the enticements of hope, the solicitations of affection, the importunities of appetite, or the depressions of fear, and is in the same state with him that teaches upon land the art of navigation, to whom the sea is always smooth, and the wind always prosperous.

The mathematicians are well acquainted with the difference between pure science, which has to do only with ideas, and the application of its laws to the use of life, in which they are constrained to submit to the imperfection of matter and the influence of accidents. Thus, in moral discussions it is to be remembred that many impediments obstruct our practice, which very easily give way to theory. The speculatist is only in danger of erroneous reasoning, but the man involved in life has his own passions, and those of others, to encounter, and is embarrassed with a thousand inconveniences, which confound him with variety of impulse, and either perplex or obstruct his way. He is forced to act without deliberation, and obliged to choose before he can examine; he is surprised by sudden alterations of the state of things, and changes his measures according to superficial appearances; he is led by others, either because he is indolent, or because he is timorous; he is sometimes afraid to know what is right, and sometimes finds friends or enemies diligent to deceive him.

We are, therefore, not to wonder that most fail, amidst tumult, and snares, and danger, in the observance of those precepts, which they laid down in solitude, safety, and tranquillity, with a mind unbiassed, and with liberty unobstructed. It is the condition of our present state to see more than we can attain, the exactest vigilance and caution can never maintain a single day of unmingled innocence, much less can the utmost efforts of incorporated mind reach the summits of speculative virtue.

It is, however, necessary for the idea of perfection to be proposed, that we may have some object to which our endeavours are to be directed; and he that is most deficient in the duties of life, makes some atonement for his faults, if he warns others against his own failings, and hinders, by the salubrity of his admonitions, the contagion of his example.

Nothing is more unjust, however common, than to charge with hypocrisy him that expresses zeal for those virtues, which he neglects to practise; since he may be sincerely convinced of the advantages of conquering his passions, without having yet obtained the victory, as a man may be confident of the advantages of a voyage, or a journey, without having courage or industry to undertake it, and may honestly recommend to others, those attempts which he neglects himself.

The interest which the corrupt part of mankind have in hardening themselves against every motive to amendment, has disposed them to give to these contradictions, when they can be produced against the cause of virtue, that weight which they will not allow them in any other case. They see men act in opposition to their interest, without supposing, that they do not know it; those who give way to the sudden violence of passion, and forsake the most important persuits for petty pleasures, are not supposed to have changed their opinions, or to approve their own conduct. In moral or religious questions alone, they determine the sentiments by the actions, and charge every man with endeavouring to impose upon the world, whose writings are not confirmed by his life. They never consider that they themselves neglect, or practise something every day, inconsistently with their own settled judgment, nor discover that the conduct of the advocates for virtue can little increase, or lessen, the obligations of their dictates; argument is to be invalidated only by argument, and is in itself of the same force, whether or not it convinces him by whom it is proposed.

Yet since this prejudice, however unreasonable, is always likely to have some prevalence, it is the duty of every man to take care lest he should hinder the efficacy of his own instructions. When he desires to gain the belief of others, he should shew that he believes himself; and when he teaches the fitness of virtue by his reasonings, he should, by his example, prove its possibility: Thus much at least may be required of him, that he shall not act worse than others because he writes better, nor imagine that, by the merit of his genius, he may claim indulgence beyond mortals of the lower classes, and be excused for want of prudence, or neglect of virtue.

BACON, in his History of the winds, after having offered something to the imagination as desirable, often proposes lower advantages in its place to the reason as attainable. The same method may be sometimes pursued in moral endeavours, which this philosopher has observed in natural enquiries; having first set positive and absolute excellence before us, we may be pardoned though we sink down to humbler virtue, trying, however, to keep our point always in view, and struggling not to lose ground, though we cannot gain it.

It is recorded of Sir Matthew Hale, that he, for a long time, concealed the consecration of himself to the stricter duties of religion, lest, by some flagitious and shameful action, he should bring piety into disgrace. For the same reason, it may be prudent for a writer, who apprehends that he shall not inforce his own maxims by his domestic character, to conceal his name that he may not injure them.

There are, indeed, a greater number whose curiosity to gain a more familiar knowledge of successful writers, is not so much prompted by an opinion of their power to improve as to delight, and who expect from them not arguments against vice, or dissertations on temperance or justice, but flights of wit, and sallies of pleasantry, or, at least, acute remarks, nice distinctions, justness of sentiment, and elegance of diction.

This expectation is, indeed, specious and probable, and yet, such is the fate of all human hopes, that it is very often frustrated, and those who raise admiration by their books, disgust by their company. A man of letters for the most part spends, in the privacies of study, that season of life in which the manners are to be softened into ease, and polished into elegance, and, when he has gained knowledge enough to be respected, has neglected the minuter acts by which he might have pleased. When he enters life, if his temper be soft and timorous, he is diffident and bashful, from the knowledge of his defects; or if he was born with spirit and resolution, he is ferocious and arrogant from the consciousness of his merit: he is either dissipated by the awe of company, and unable to recollect his reading, and arrange his arguments; or he is hot, and dogmatical, quick in opposition, and tenacious in defence, disabled by his own violence, and confused by his haste to triumph.

The graces of writing and conversation are of different kinds, and though he who excels in one might have been with opportunities and application equally successful in the other, yet as many please by extempory talk, though utterly unacquainted with the more accurate method, and more laboured beauties, which composition requires; so it is very possible that men, wholly accustomed to works of study, may be without that readiness of conception, and affluence of language, always necessary to colloquial entertainment. They may want address to watch the hints which conversation offers for the display of their particular attainments, or they may be so much unfurnished with matter on common subjects, that discourse not professedly literary glides over them as heterogeneous bodies, without admitting their conceptions to mix in the circulation.

A transition from an author's books to his conversation, is too often like an entrance into a large city, after a distant prospect. Remotely, we see nothing but spires of temples, and turrets of palaces, and imagine it the residence of splendor, grandeur, and magnificence; but, when we have passed the gates, we find it perplexed with narrow passages, disgraced with despicable cottages, embarrassed with obstructions, and clouded with smoke.

The Benefits of Human Society

Inventas—vitam excoluere per artes.

Virg.

They polish life by useful arts.

That familiarity produces neglect, has been long observed. The effect of all external objects, however great
or splendid, ceases with their novelty: the courtier stands
without emotion in the royal presence; the rustic
tramples under his foot the beauties of the spring, with
little attention to their colour or their fragrance; and the
inhabitant of the coast darts his eye upon the immense
diffusion of waters, without awe, wonder, or terror.

Those who have past much of their lives in this great
city, look upon its opulence and its multitudes, its extent
and variety, with cold indifference; but an inhabitant
of the remoter parts of the kingdom is immediately
distinguished by a kind of dissipated curiosity, a busy
endeavour to divide his attention amongst a thousand
objects, and a wild confusion of astonishment and alarm.

The attention of a new-comer is generally first struck
by the multiplicity of cries that stun him in the streets,
and the variety of merchandise and manufactures which
the shopkeepers expose on every hand; and he is apt, by

unwary bursts of admiration, to excite the merriment and contempt of those, who mistake the use of their eyes for effects of their understanding, and confound accidental knowledge with just reasoning.

But, surely, these are subjects on which any man may without reproach employ his meditations: the innumerable occupations, among which the thousands that swarm in the streets of London are distributed, may furnish employment to minds of every cast, and capacities of every degree. He that contemplates the extent of this wonderful city, finds it difficult to conceive, by what method plenty is maintained in our markets, and how the inhabitants are regularly supplied with the necessaries of life; but when he examines the shops and warehouses, sees the immense stores of every kind of merchandise piled up for sale, and runs over all the manufactures of art and products of nature, which are every where attracting his eye and solliciting his purse, he will be inclined to conclude, that such quantities cannot easily be exhausted, and that part of mankind must soon stand still for want of employment, till the wares already provided shall be worn out and destroyed.

As SOCRATES was passing through the fair at Athens, and casting his eyes over the shops and customers, 'how many things are here,' says he, 'that I do not want!' The same sentiment is every moment rising in the mind of him that walks the streets of London, however inferior in philosophy to SOCRATES: he beholds a thousand shops crouded with goods, of which he can scarcely tell the use, and which, therefore, he is apt to consider as of no value; and, indeed, many of the arts by which families are supported, and wealth is heaped together, are of that minute and superfluous kind, which nothing but experience could evince possible to be prosecuted with advantage, and which, as the world might easily want, it could scarcely be expected to encourage.

But so it is, that custom, curiosity, or wantonness, supplies every art with patrons, and finds purchasers for every manufacture; the world is so adjusted, that not only bread, but riches may be obtained without great abilities, or arduous performances: the most unskilful hand and unenlightened mind have sufficient incitements to industry; for he that is resolutely busy, can scarcely be in want. There is, indeed, no employment, however despicable, from which a man may not promise himself more than competence, when he sees thousands and myriads raised to dignity, by no other merit than that of contributing to supply their neighbours with the means of sucking smoke through a tube of clay; and others raising contributions upon those, whose elegance disdains the grossness of smoky luxury, by grinding the same materials into a powder, that may at once gratify and impair the smell.

Not only by these popular and modish trifles, but by a thousand unheeded and evanescent kinds of business, are the multitudes of this city preserved from idleness, and consequently from want. In the endless variety of tastes and circumstances that diversify mankind, nothing is so superfluous, but that some one desires it; or so common, but that some one is compelled to buy it. As nothing is useless but because it is in improper hands, what is thrown away by one is gathered up by another; and the refuse of part of mankind furnishes a subordinate class with the materials necessary to their support.

When I look round upon those who are thus variously exerting their qualifications, I cannot but admire the secret concatenation of society, that links together the great and the mean, the illustrious and the obscure; and consider with benevolent satisfaction, that no man, unless his body or mind be totally disabled, has need to suffer the mortification of seeing himself useless or burdensome to the community: he that will diligently labour, in whatever occupation, will deserve the sustenance which he obtains, and the protection which he enjoys; and may lie down every night with the pleasing consciousness, of having contributed something to the happiness of life.

Contempt and admiration are equally incident to narrow minds: he whose comprehension can take in the whole subordination of mankind, and whose perspicacity can pierce to the real state of things through the thin veils of fortune or of fashion, will discover meanness in the highest stations, and dignity in the meanest; and find that no man can become venerable but by virtue, or contemptible but by wickedness.

In the midst of this universal hurry, no man ought to be so little influenced by example, or so void of honest emulation, as to stand a lazy spectator of incessant labour; or please himself with the mean happiness of a drone, while the active swarms are buzzing about him: no man is without some quality, by the due application of which he might deserve well of the world; and whoever he be that has but little in his power, should be in haste to do that little, lest he be confounded with him that can do nothing.

By this general concurrence of endeavours, arts of every kind have been so long cultivated, that all the wants of man may be immediately supplied; idleness can scarcely form a wish which she may not gratify by the toil of others, or curiosity dream of a toy which the shops are not ready to afford her.

Happiness is enjoyed only in proportion as it is known; and such is the state or folly of man, that it is known only by experience of its contrary: we who have long lived amidst the conveniences of a town immensely populous, have scarce an idea of a place where desire cannot be gratified by money. In order to have a just sense of this artificial plenty, it is necessary to have passed some time in a distant colony, or those parts of our island which are thinly inhabited: he that has once known how many trades every man in such situations is compelled to exercise, with how much labour the products of nature must be accommodated to human use, how long the loss or defect of any common utensil must be endured, or by what aukward expedients it must be supplied, how far men may wander with money in their hands before any can sell them what they wish to buy, will know how to rate at its proper value the plenty and ease of a great city.

But that the happiness of man may still remain imperfect, as wants in this place are easily supplied, new wants likewise are easily created: every man, in surveying the shops of London, sees numberless instruments and conveniences, of which, while he did not know them, he never felt the need; and yet, when use has made them familiar, wonders how life could be supported without them. Thus it comes to pass, that our desires always increase with our possessions; the knowledge that something remains yet unenjoyed, impairs our enjoyment of the good before us.

They who have been accustomed to the refinements of science, and multiplications of contrivance, soon lose their confidence in the unassisted powers of nature, forget the paucity of our real necessities, and overlook the easy methods by which they may be supplied. It were a speculation worthy of a philosophical mind, to examine how much is taken away from our native abilities, as well as added to them by artificial expedients. We are so accustomed to give and receive assistance, that each of us singly can do little for himself; and there is scarce any one amongst us, however contracted may be his form of life, who does not enjoy the labour of a thousand artists.

But a survey of the various nations that inhabit the earth will inform us, that life may be supported with less assistance, and that the dexterity, which practice enforced by necessity produces, is able to effect much by very scanty means. The nations of Mexico and Peru erected cities and temples without the use of iron; and at this day the rude Indian supplies himself with all the necessaries of life: sent like the rest of mankind naked into the world, as soon as his parents have nursed him up to strength, he is to provide by his own labour for his own support. His first care is to find a sharp flint among the rocks; with this he undertakes to fell the trees of the forest; he shapes his bow, heads his arrows, builds his cottage, and hollows his canoe, and from that time lives in a state of plenty and prosperity; he is sheltered from the storms, he is fortified against beasts of prey, he is enabled to persue the fish of the sea, and the deer of the mountains; and as he does not know, does not envy the happiness of polished nations, where gold can supply the want of fortitude and skill, and he whose laborious ancestors have made him rich, may lie stretched upon a couch, and see all the treasures of all the elements poured down before him.

This picture of a savage life, if it shews how much individuals may perform, shews likewise how much society is to be desired. Though the perseverance and address of the Indian excite our admiration, they nevertheless cannot procure him the conveniences which are enjoyed by the vagrant begger of a civilized country: he hunts like a wild beast to satisfy his hunger; and when he lies down to rest after a successful chace, cannot pronounce himself secure against the danger of perishing in a few days; he is, perhaps, content with his condition, because he knows not that a better is attainable by man; as he that is born blind does not long for the perception of light, because he cannot conceive the advantages which light would afford him: but hunger, wounds and weariness are real evils, though he believes them equally incident to all his fellow creatures; and when a tempest compels him to lie starving in his hut, he cannot justly be concluded equally happy with those whom art has exempted from the power of chance, and who make the foregoing year provide for the following.

To receive and to communicate assistance, constitutes the happiness of human life: man may indeed preserve his existence in solitude, but can enjoy it only in society: the greatest understanding of an individual, doomed to procure food and cloathing for himself, will barely supply him with expedients to keep off death from day to day; but as one of a large community performing only his share of the common business, he gains leisure for intellectual pleasures, and enjoys the happiness of reason and reflection.

The Role of the Scholar

Qui cupit optatam cursu contingere metam,
Multa tulit fecitque puer.

HOR.

The youth, who hopes th' Olympic prize to gain,
All arts must try, and every toil sustain.

FRANCIS.

It is observed by BACON that 'reading makes a full man, conversation a ready man, and writing an exact man.'

As BACON attained to degrees of knowledge scarcely ever reached by any other man, the directions which he gives for study, have certainly a just claim to our regard; for who can teach an art with so great authority, as he that has practised it with undisputed success?

Under the protection of so great a name, I shall, therefore, venture to inculcate to my ingenious contemporaries, the necessity of reading, the fitness of consulting other understandings than their own, and of considering the sentiments and opinions of those who, however neglected in the present age, had in their own times, and many of them a long time afterwards, such reputation for knowledge and acuteness, as will scarcely ever be attained by those that despise them.

An opinion has of late been, I know not how, propagated among us, that libraries are filled only with useless lumber; that men of parts stand in need of no assistance; and that to spend life in poring upon books, is only to imbibe prejudices, to obstruct and embarrass the powers of nature, to cultivate memory at the expence of judgement, and to bury reason under a chaos of indigested learning.

Such is the talk of many who think themselves wise, and of some who are thought wise by others; of whom part probably believe their own tenets, and part may be justly suspected of endeavouring to shelter their ignorance in multitudes, and of wishing to destroy that reputation which they have no hopes to share. It will, I believe, be found invariably true, that learning was never decried by any learned man; and what credit can be given to those, who venture to condemn that which they do not know?

If reason has the power ascribed to it by its advocates, if so much is to be discovered by attention and meditation, it is hard to believe, that so many millions, equally participating of the bounties of nature with ourselves, have been for ages upon ages meditating in vain: if the wits of the present time expect the regard of posterity, which will then inherit the reason which is now thought superior to instruction, surely they may allow themselves to be instructed by the reason of former generations. When, therefore, an author declares, that he has been able to learn nothing from the writings of his predecessors, and such a declaration has been lately made, nothing but a degree of arrogance unpardonable in the greatest human understanding, can hinder him from perceiving, that he is raising prejudices against his own performance; for with what hopes of success can he attempt that in which greater abilities have hitherto miscarried? or with what peculiar force does he suppose himself invigorated, that difficulties hitherto invincible should give way before him?

Of those whom PROVIDENCE has qualified to make any additions to human knowledge, the number is extremely small; and what can be added by each single mind, even of this superior class, is very little: the greatest part of mankind must owe all their knowledge, and all must owe far the larger part of it, to the information of others. To understand the works of celebrated authors, to comprehend their systems, and retain their reasonings, is a task more than equal to common intellects; and he is by no means to be accounted useless or idle, who has stored his mind with acquired knowledge, and can detail it occasionally to others who have less leisure or weaker abilities.

PERSIUS has justly observed, that knowledge is nothing to him who is not known by others to possess it: to the scholar himself it is nothing with respect either to honour or advantage, for the world cannot reward those qualities which are concealed from it; with respect to others it is nothing, because it affords no help to ignorance or error.

It is with justice, therefore, that in an accomplished character, HORACE unites just sentiments with the power of expressing them; and he that has once accumulated learning, is next to consider, how he shall most widely diffuse and most agreeably impart it.

A ready man is made by conversation. He that buries himself among his manuscripts 'besprent,' as POPE expresses it, 'with learned dust,' and wears out his days and nights in perpetual research and solitary meditation, is too apt to lose in his elocution what he adds to his wisdom, and when he comes into the world, to appear overloaded with his own notions, like a man armed with weapons which he cannot wield. He has no facility of inculcating his speculations, of adapting himself to the various degrees of intellect which the accidents of conversation will present; but will talk to most unintelligibly, and to all unpleasantly.

I was once present at the lectures of a profound philosopher, a man really skilled in the science which he professed, who having occasion to explain the terms OPACUM and PELLUCIDUM, told us, after some hesitation, that OPACUM was as one might say OPAKE, and that PELLUCIDUM signified PELLUCID. Such was the dexterity, with which this learned reader facilitated to his auditors the intricacies of science; and so true is it, that a man may know what he cannot teach.

BOERHAAVE complains, that the writers who have treated of chemistry before him, are useless to the greater part of students; because they presuppose their readers to have such degrees of skill as are not often to be found. Into the same error are all men apt to fall, who have familiarized any subject to themselves in solitude: they discourse, as if they thought every other man had been employed in the same inquiries; and expect that short hints and obscure allusions will produce in others, the same train of ideas which they excite in themselves.

Nor is this the only inconvenience which the man of study suffers from a recluse life. When he meets with an opinion that pleases him, he catches it up with eagerness; looks only after such arguments as tend to his confirmation; or spares himself the trouble of discussion, and adopts it with very little proof; indulges it long without suspicion, and in time unites it to the general body of his knowledge, and treasures it up among incontestible truths: but when he comes into the world among men who, arguing upon dissimilar principles, have been led to different conclusions, and being placed in various situations view the same object on many sides; he finds his darling position attacked, and himself in no condition to defend it: having thought always in one train, he is in the state of a man who having fenced always with the same master, is perplexed and amazed by a new posture of his antagonist; he is entangled in unexpected difficulties, he is harrassed by sudden objections, he is unprovided with solutions or replies, his surprize impedes his natural powers of reasoning, his thoughts are scattered and confounded, and he gratifies the pride of airy petulance with an easy victory.

It is difficult to imagine, with what obstinacy truths which one mind perceives almost by intuition, will be rejected by another; and how many artifices must be practised, to procure admission for the most evident propositions into understandings frighted by their novelty, or hardened against them by accidental prejudice: it can scarcely be conceived, how frequently in these extemporaneous controversies, the dull will be subtle, and the acute absurd; how often stupidity will elude the force of argument, by involving itself in its own gloom; and mistaken ingenuity will weave artful fallacies, which reason can scarcely find means to disentangle.

In these encounters the learning of the recluse usually fails him: nothing but long habit and frequent experiments can confer the power of changing a position into various forms, presenting it in different points of view, connecting it with known and granted truths, fortifying it with intelligible arguments, and illustrating it by apt similitudes; and he, therefore, that has collected his knowledge in solitude, must learn its application by mixing with mankind.

But while the various opportunities of conversation invite us to try every mode of argument, and every art of recommending our sentiments, we are frequently betrayed to the use of such as are not in themselves strictly defensible: a man heated in talk, and eager of victory, takes advantage of the mistakes or ignorance of his adversary, lays hold of concessions to which he knows he has no right, and urges proofs likely to prevail on his opponent, though he knows himself that they have no force: thus the severity of reason is relaxed; many topics are accumulated, but without just arrangement or distinction; we learn to satisfy ourselves with such ratiocination as silences others; and seldom recall to a close examination, that discourse which has gratified our vanity with victory and applause.

Some caution, therefore, must be used, lest copiousness and facility be made less valuable by inaccuracy and confusion. To fix the thoughts by writing, and subject them to frequent examinations and reviews, is the best method of enabling the mind to detect its own sophisms, and keep it on guard against the fallacies which it practices on others: in conversation we naturally diffuse our thoughts, and in writing we contract them; method is the excellence of writing, and unconstraint the grace of conversation.

To read, write, and converse in due proportions, is, therefore, the business of a man of letters. For all these there is not often equal opportunity; excellence, therefore, is not often attainable; and most men fail in one or other of the ends proposed, and are full without readiness, or ready without exactness. Some deficiency must be forgiven all, because all are men; and more must be allowed to pass uncensured in the greater part of the world, because none can confer upon himself abilities, and few have the choice of situations proper for the improvement of those which nature has bestowed: it is, however, reasonable, to have PERFECTION in our eye; that we may always advance towards it, though we know it never can be reached.

Observations on the present State of Affairs (1756)

The time is now come in which every *Englishman* expects
to be informed of the national affairs, and in which he
has a right to have that expectation gratified. For whatever may be urged by ministers, or those whom vanity
or interest make the followers of ministers, concerning the necessity of confidence in our governors, and
the presumption of prying with profane eyes into the
recesses of policy, it is evident, that this reverence can
be claimed only by counsels yet unexecuted, and projects
suspended in deliberation. But when a design has ended
in miscarriage or success, when every eye and every ear
is witness to general discontent, or general satisfaction,
it is then a proper time to disintangle confusion and
illustrate obscurity, to shew by what causes every event
was produced, and in what effects it is likely to terminate:
to lay down with distinct particularity what rumour
always huddles in general exclamations, or perplexes by
undigested narratives; to shew whence happiness or
calamity is derived, and whence it may be expected, and
honestly to lay before the people what inquiry can gather
of the past, and conjecture can estimate of the future.

The general subject of the present war is sufficiently
known. It is allowed on both sides, that hostilities began
in *America*, and that the *French* and *English* quarrelled about
the boundaries of their settlements, about grounds and

rivers to which, I am afraid, neither can shew any other right than that of power, and which neither can occupy but by usurpation, and the dispossession of the natural lords and original inhabitants. Such is the contest that no honest man can heartily wish success to either party.

It may indeed be alleged, that the Indians have granted large tracts of land both to one and to the other; but these grants can add little to the validity of our titles, till it be experienced how they were obtained: for if they were extorted by violence, or induced by fraud; by threats, which the miseries of other nations had shewn not to be vain, or by promises of which no performance was ever intended, what are they but new modes of usurpation, but new instances of cruelty and treachery?

And indeed what but false hope, or resistless terror can prevail upon a weaker nation to invite a stronger into their country, to give their lands to strangers whom no affinity of manners, or similitude of opinion can be said to recommend, to permit them to build towns from which the natives are excluded, to raise fortresses by which they are intimidated, to settle themselves with such strength, that they cannot afterwards be expelled, but are for ever to remain the masters of the original inhabitants, the dictators of their conduct, and the arbiters of their fate?

When we see men acting thus against the precepts of reason, and the instincts of nature, we cannot hesitate to determine, that by some means or other they were debarred from choice; that they were lured or frighted into compliance; that they either granted only what they found impossible to keep, or expected advantages upon the faith of their new inmates, which there was no purpose to confer upon them. It cannot be said, that the Indians originally invited us to their coasts; we went uncalled and unexpected to nations who had no imagination that the earth contained any inhabitants so distant and so different from themselves. We astonished them with our ships, with our arms, and with our general superiority. They yielded to us as to beings of another and higher race, sent among them from some unknown regions, with power which naked Indians could not resist, and which they were therefore, by every act of humility, to propitiate, that they, who could so easily destroy, might be induced to spare.

To this influence, and to this only, are to be attributed all the cessions and submissions of the Indian princes, if indeed any such cessions were ever made, of which we have no witness but those who claim from them, and there is no great malignity in suspecting, that those who have robbed have also lied.

Some colonies indeed have been established more peaceably than others. The utmost extremity of wrong has not always been practised; but those that have settled in the new world on the fairest terms, have no other merit than that of a scrivener who ruins in silence over a plunderer that seizes by force; all have taken what had other owners, and all have had recourse to arms, rather than quit the prey on which they had fastened.

The *American* dispute between the *French* and us is therefore only the quarrel of two robbers for the spoils of a passenger, but as robbers have terms of confederacy, which they are obliged to observe as members of the gang, so the *English* and *French* may have relative rights, and do injustice to each other, while both are injuring the Indians. And such, indeed, is the present contest: they have parted the northern continent of *America* between them, and are now disputing about their boundaries, and each is endeavouring the destruction of the other by the help of the Indians, whose interest it is that both should be destroyed.

Both nations clamour with great vehemence about infraction of limits, violation of treaties, open usurpation, insidious artifices, and breach of faith. The *English* rail at the perfidious *French*, and the *French* at the encroaching *English*; they quote treaties on each side, charge each other with aspiring to universal monarchy, and complain on either part of the insecurity of possession near such turbulent neighbours.

Through this mist of controversy it can raise no wonder, that the truth is not easily discovered. When a quarrel has been long carried on between individuals, it is often very hard to tell by whom it was begun. Every fact is darkened by distance, by interest, and by multitudes. Information is not easily procured from far; those whom the truth will not favour, will not step voluntarily forth to tell it, and where there are many agents, it is easy for every single action to be concealed.

All these causes concur to the obscurity of the question, by whom were hostilities in *America* commenced? Perhaps there never can be remembered a time in which hostilities had ceased. Two powerful colonies enflamed with immemorial rivalry, and placed out of the superintendence of the mother nations, were not likely to be long at rest. Some opposition was always going forward, some mischief was every day done or meditated, and the borderers were always better pleased with what they could snatch from their neighbours, than what they had of their own.

In this disposition to reciprocal invasion a cause of dispute never could be wanting. The forests and desarts of *America* are without land-marks, and therefore cannot be particularly specified in stipulations; the appellations of those wide extended regions have in every mouth a different meaning, and are understood on either side as inclination happens to contract or extend them. Who has yet pretended to define how much of *America* is included in *Brazil, Mexico,* or *Peru*? It is almost as easy to divide the *Atlantic* ocean by a line as clearly to ascertain the limits of those uncultivated, uninhabitable, unmeasured regions.

It is likewise to be considered, that contracts concerning boundaries are often left vague and indefinite without necessity, by the desire of each party, to interpret the ambiguity to its own advantage when a fit opportunity shall be found. In forming stipulations, the commissaries are often ignorant, and often negligent; they are sometimes weary with debate, and contract a tedious discussion into general terms, or refer it to a former treaty, which was never understood. The weaker part is always afraid of requiring explanations, and the stronger always has an interest in leaving the question undecided: thus it will happen without great caution on either side, that after long treaties solemnly ratified, the rights that had been disputed are still equally open to controversy.

In *America* it may easily be supposed, that there are tracts of land yet claimed by neither party, and therefore mentioned in no treaties, which yet one or the other may be afterwards inclined to occupy; but to these vacant and unsettled countries each nation may pretend, as each conceives itself intitled to all that is not expressly granted to the other.

Here then is a perpetual ground of contest, every enlargement of the possessions of either will be considered as something taken from the other, and each will endeavour to regain what had never been claimed, but that the other occupied it.

Thus obscure in its original is the *American* contest. It is difficult to find the first invader, or to tell where invasion properly begins; but I suppose it is not to be doubted, that after the last war, when the *French* had made peace with such apparent superiority, they naturally began to treat us with less respect in distant parts of the world, and to consider us as a people from whom they had nothing to fear, and who could no longer presume to contravene their designs, or to check their progress.

The power of doing wrong with impunity seldom waits long for the will, and it is reasonable to believe, that in *America* the *French* would avow their purpose of aggrandising themselves with at least as little reserve as in *Europe*. We may therefore readily believe, that they were unquiet neighbours, and had no great regard to right which they believed us no longer able to enforce.

That in forming a line of forts behind our colonies, if in no other part of their attempt, they had acted against the general intention, if not against the literal terms of treaties, can scarcely be denied; for it never can be supposed, that we intended to be inclosed between the sea and the *French* garrisons, or preclude ourselves from extending our plantations backwards to any length that our convenience should require.

With dominion is conferred every thing that can secure dominion. He that has the coast has likewise the sea to a certain distance; he that possesses a fortress, has the right of prohibiting another fortress to be built within the command of its cannon. When therefore we planted the coast of *North-America* we supposed the possession of the inland region granted to an indefinite extent, and every nation that settled in that part of the world, seems, by the permission of every other nation, to have made the same supposition in its own favour.

Here then, perhaps, it will be safest to fix the justice of our cause; here we are apparently and indisputably injured, and this injury may, according to the practice of nations, be justly resented. Whether we have not in return made some incroachments upon them, must be left doubtful, till our practices on the *Ohio* shall be stated and vindicated. There are no two nations confining on each other, between whom a war may not always be kindled with plausible pretences on either part, as there is always passing between them a reciprocation of injuries and fluctuation of incroachments.

From the conclusion of the last peace perpetual complaints of the supplantations and invasions of the *French* have been sent to *Europe* from our colonies, and transmitted to our ministers at *Paris*, where good words were sometimes given us, and the practices of the *American* commanders were sometimes disowned, but no redress was ever obtained, nor is it probable that any prohibition was sent to *America*. We were still amused with such doubtful promises as those who are afraid of war are ready to interpret in their own favour, and the *French* pushed forward their line of fortresses, and seemed to resolve that before our complaints were finally dismissed, all remedy should be hopeless.

We likewise endeavour'd at the same time to form a barrier against the *Canadians* by sending a colony to *New-Scotland*, a cold uncomfortable tract of ground, of which we had long the nominal possession before we really began to occupy it. To this those were invited whom the cessation of war deprived of employment, and made burdensom to their country, and settlers were allured thither by many fallacious descriptions of fertile vallies and clear skies. What effect these pictures of *American* happiness had upon my countrymen I was never informed, but I suppose very few sought provision in those frozen regions, whom guilt or poverty did not drive from their native country. About the boundaries of this new colony there were some disputes, but as there was nothing yet worth a contest, the power of the *French* was not much exerted on that side: some disturbance was however given and some skirmishes ensued. But perhaps being peopled chiefly with soldiers, who would rather live by plunder than by agriculture, and who consider war as their best trade, *New-Scotland* would be more obstinately defended than some settlements of far greater value, and the *French* are too well informed of their own interest, to provoke hostility for no advantage, or to select that country for invasion, where they must hazard much, and can win little. They therefore pressed on southward behind our ancient and wealthy settlements, and built fort after fort at such distances that they might conveniently relieve one another, invade our colonies with sudden incursions, and retire to places of safety before our people could unite to oppose them.

This design of the *French* has been long formed, and long known, both in *America* and *Europe*, and might at first have been easily repressed had force been used instead of expostulation. When the *English* attempted a settlement upon the Island of St. *Lucia*, the *French*, whether justly or not, considering it as neutral and forbidden to be occupied by either nation, immediately landed upon it, and destroyed the houses, wasted the plantations, and drove or carried away the inhabitants. This was done in the time of peace, when mutual professions of friendship were daily exchanged by the two courts, and was not considered as any violation of treaties, nor was any more than a very soft remonstrance made on our part.

The *French* therefore taught us how to act, but an *Hanoverian* quarrel with the house of *Austria* for some time induced us to court, at any expence, the alliance of a nation whose very situation makes them our enemies. We suffered them to destroy our settlements, and to advance their own, which we had an equal right to attack. The time however came at last, when we ventured to quarrel with *Spain*, and then *France* no longer suffered the appearance of peace to subsist between us, but armed in defence of her ally.

The events of the war are well known, we pleased ourselves with victory at *Dettingen*, where we left our wounded men to the care of our enemies, but our army was broken at *Fontenoy* and *Val*; and though after the disgrace which we suffered in the *Mediterranean* we had some naval success, and an accidental dearth made peace necessary for the *French*, yet they prescribed the conditions, obliged us to give hostages, and acted as conquerors, though as conquerors of moderation.

In this war the *Americans* distinguished themselves in a manner unknown and unexpected. The *New English* raised an army, and under the command of *Pepperel* took *Cape-Breton*, with the assistance of the fleet. This is the most important fortress in *America*. We pleased ourselves so much with the acquisition, that we could not think of restoring it, and among the arguments used to inflame the people against *Charles Stuart*, it was very clamorously urged, that if he gained the kingdom, he would give *Cape-Breton* back to the *French*.

The *French* however had a more easy expedient to regain *Cape-Breton* than by exalting *Charles Stuart* to the *English* throne; they took in their turn fort *St. George*, and had our *East-India* company wholly in their power, whom they restored at the peace to their former possessions, that they may continue to export our silver.

Cape-Breton therefore was restored, and the *French* were re-established in *America*, with equal power and greater spirit, having lost nothing by the war which they had before gained.

To the general reputation of their arms, and that habitual superiority which they derive from it, they owe their power in *America*, rather than to any real strength, or circumstances of advantage. Their numbers are yet not great; their trade, though daily improved, is not very extensive; their country is barren, their fortresses, though numerous, are weak, and rather shelters from wild beasts, or savage nations, than places built for defence against bombs or cannons. *Cape-Breton* has been found not to be impregnable; nor, if we consider the state of the places possessed by the two nations in *America*, is there any reason upon which the *French* should have presumed to molest us but that they thought our spirit so broken that we durst not resist them, and in this opinion our long forbearance easily confirmed them.

We forgot, or rather avoided to think, that what we delayed to do must be done at last, and done with more difficulty, as it was delayed longer; that while we were complaining, and they were eluding, or answering our complaints, fort was rising upon fort, and one invasion made a precedent for another.

This confidence of the *French* is exalted by some real advantages. If they possess in those countries less than we, they have more to gain, and less to hazard; if they are less numerous, they are better united.

The *French* compose one body with one head. They have all the same interest, and agree to pursue it by the same means. They are subject to a governor commission'd by an absolute monarch, and participating the authority of his master. Designs are therefore formed without debate, and executed without impediment.

They have yet more martial than mercantile ambition, and seldom suffer their military schemes to be entangled with collateral projects of gain: they have no wish but for conquest, of which they justly consider riches as the consequence.

Some advantages they will always have as invaders. They make war at the hazard of their enemies: the contest being carried on in our territories we must lose more by a victory than they will suffer by a defeat. They will subsist, while they stay, upon our plantations, and perhaps destroy them when they can stay no longer. If we pursue them and carry the war into their dominions, our difficulties will encrease every step as we advance, for we shall leave plenty behind us, and find nothing in *Canada*, but lakes and forests barren and trackless, our enemies will shut themselves up in their forts, against which it is difficult to bring cannon through so rough a country, and which if they are provided with good magazines will soon starve those who besiege them.

All these are the natural effects of their government, and situation; they are accidentally more formidable as they are less happy. But the favour of the Indians which they enjoy, with very few exceptions, among all the nations of the northern continent, we ought to consider with other thoughts; this favour we might have enjoyed, if we had been careful to deserve it. The *French* by having these savage nations on their side, are always supplied with spies, and guides, and with auxiliaries, like the *Tartars* to the *Turks* or the Hussars to the *Germans*, of no great use against troops ranged in order of battle, but very well qualified to maintain a war among woods and rivulets, where much mischief may be done by unexpected onsets, and safety be obtained by quick retreats. They can waste a colony by sudden inroads, surprise the straggling planters, frighten the inhabitants into towns, hinder the cultivation of lands, and starve those whom they are not able to conquer.

(To be continued.)

Of the Duty of a Journalist

It is an unpleasing consideration that Virtue cannot be inferred from Knowledge; that many can teach others those Duties which they never practise themselves; yet, tho' there may be speculative Knowledge without actual Performance, there can be no Performance without Knowledge; and the present state of many of our Papers is such that it may be doubted not only whether the Compilers know their Duty, but whether they have endeavoured or wished to know it.

A Journalist is an Historian, not indeed of the highest Class, nor of the number of those whose works bestow immortality upon others or themselves; yet, like other Historians, he distributes for a time Reputation or Infamy, regulates the opinion of the week, raises hopes and terrors, inflames or allays the violence of the people. He ought therefore to consider himself as subject at least to the first law of History, the Obligation to tell Truth. The Journalist, indeed, however honest, will frequently deceive, because he will frequently be deceived himself. He is obliged to transmit the earliest intelligence before he knows how far it may be credited; he relates transactions yet fluctuating in uncertainty; he delivers reports of which he knows not the Authors. It cannot be expected that he should know more than he is told, or that he should not sometimes be hurried down the current of a popular clamour. All that he can do is to consider attentively, and determine impartially, to admit no false-hoods by design, and to retract those which he shall have adopted by mistake.

This is not much to be required, and yet this is more than the Writers of News seem to exact from themselves. It must surely sometimes raise indignation to observe with what serenity of confidence they relate on one day, what they know not to be true, because they hope that it will please; and with what shameless tranquillity they contradict it on the next day, when they find that it will please no longer. How readily they receive any report that will disgrace our enemies, and how eagerly they accumulate praises upon a name, which caprice or acci-dent has made a Favourite. They know, by experience, however destitute of reason, that what is desired will be credited without nice examination: they do not therefore always limit their narratives by possibility, but slaughter armies without battles, and conquer countries without invasions.

There are other violations of truth admitted only to gratify idle curiosity, which yet are mischievous in their consequences, and hateful in their contrivance. Accounts are sometimes published of robberies and murders which never were committed, men's minds are terrified with fictitious dangers, the publick indignation is raised, and the Government of our country depreciated and con-temned. These Scriblers, who give false alarms, ought to be taught, by some public animadversion, that to relate crimes is to teach them, and that as most men are content to follow the herd, and to be like their neighbours,

nothing contributes more to the frequency of wickedness, than the representation of it as already frequent.

There is another practice, of which the injuriousness
is more apparent, and which, if the law could succour
the Poor, is now punishable by law. The Advertisement
of Apprentices who have left their Masters, and who are
often driven away by cruelty or hunger; the minute
descriptions of men whom the law has not considered
as criminal, and the insinuations often published in such
a manner, that, though obscure to the publick, they are
well understood where they can do most mischief; and
many other practices by which particular interests are
injured, are to be diligently avoided by an honest Journalist, whose business is only to tell transactions of
general importance, or uncontested notoriety, or by
Advertisements to promote private convenience without
disturbance of private quiet.

Thus far the Journalist is obliged to deviate from
the common methods of his Competitors by the laws
of unvariable morality. Other improvements may be
expected from him as conducive to delight or information. It is common to find passages, in Papers of
Intelligence, which cannot be understood: Obscure
places are sometimes mentioned without any information from Geography or History. Sums of money are
reckoned by coins or denominations, of which the value
is not known in this country. Terms of war and navigation are inserted, which are utterly unintelligible to all
who are not engaged in military or naval business.
A Journalist, above most other men, ought to be
acquainted with the lower orders of mankind, that he

may be able to judge, what will be plain and what will be obscure; what will require a Comment, and what will be apprehended without Explanation. He is to consider himself not as writing to Students or Statesmen alone, but to Women, Shopkeepers, and Artisans, who have little time to bestow upon mental attainments, but desire, upon easy terms, to know how the world goes; who rises, and who falls; who triumphs, and who is defeated.

If the Writer of this Journal shall be able to execute his own Plan; if he shall carefully enquire after Truth, and diligently impart it; if he shall resolutely refuse to admit into his Paper whatever is injurious to private Reputation; if he shall relate transactions with greater clearness than others, and sell more instruction at a cheaper rate, he hopes that his labours will not be over-looked. This he promises to endeavour; and, if this Promise shall obtain the Favour of an early Attention, he desires that Favour to be continued only as it is deserved.

The Vultures' View of Man

Many naturalists are of opinion that the animals which we commonly consider as mute have the power of imparting their thoughts to one another. That they can express general sensations is very certain; every being that can utter sounds has a different voice for pleasure and for pain. The hound informs his fellows when he scents his game; the hen calls her chickens to their food by her cluck, and drives them from danger by her scream.

Birds have the greatest variety of notes; they have indeed a variety which seems almost sufficient to make a speech adequate to the purposes of a life which is regulated by instinct, and can admit little change or improvement. To the cries of birds, curiosity or superstition has been always attentive; many have studied the language of the feathered tribes, and some have boasted that they understood it.

The most skilful or most confident interpreters of the silvan dialogues have been commonly found among the philosophers of the East, in a country where the calmness of the air, and the mildness of the seasons, allow the student to pass a great part of the year in groves and bowers. But what may be done in one place by peculiar opportunities may be performed in another by peculiar diligence. A shepherd of Bohemia has, by long abode in the forests, enabled himself to understand the voice of birds; at least he relates with great confidence a story of which the credibility may be considered by the learned.

'As I was sitting,' said he, 'within a hollow rock, and watching my sheep that fed in the valley, I heard two vultures interchangeably crying on the summit of the cliff. Both voices were earnest and deliberate. My curiosity prevailed over my care of the flock; I climbed slowly and silently from crag to crag, concealed among the shrubs, till I found a cavity where I might sit and listen without suffering, or giving disturbance.

'I soon perceived that my labour would be well repaid; for an old vulture was sitting on a naked prominence, with her young about her, whom she was instructing in the arts of a vulture's life, and preparing, by the last lecture, for their final dismission to the mountains and the skies.

'"My children," said the old vulture, "you will the less want my instructions because you have had my practice before your eyes; you have seen me snatch from the farm the household fowl, you have seen me seize the leveret in the bush, and the kid in the pasture, you know how to fix your talons, and how to balance your flight when you are laden with your prey. But you remember the taste of more delicious food; I have often regaled you with the flesh of man."

'"Tell us," said the young vultures, "where man may be found, and how he may be known; his flesh is surely the natural food of a vulture. Why have you never brought a man in your talons to the nest?"

'"He is too bulky," said the mother; "when we find

a man, we can only tear away his flesh, and leave his bones upon the ground."

'"Since man is so big," said the young ones, "how do you kill him? You are afraid of the wolf and of the bear; by what power are vultures superior to man; is man more defenceless than a sheep?"

'"We have not the strength of man," returned the mother, "and I am sometimes in doubt whether we have the subtlety; and the vultures would seldom feast upon his flesh, had not Nature, that devoted him to our uses, infused into him a strange ferocity, which I have never observed in any other being that feeds upon the earth. Two herds of men will often meet and shake his earth with noise, and fill the air with fire. When you hear noise and see fire which flashes along the ground, hasten to the place with your swiftest wing, for men are surely destroying one another; you will then find the ground smoking with blood and covered with carcasses, of which many are dismembered and mangled for the convenience of the vulture."

'"But when men have killed their prey," said the pupil, "why do they not eat it? When the wolf has killed a sheep, he suffers not the vulture to touch it till he has satisfied himself. Is not man another kind of wolf?"

'"Man," said the mother, "is the only beast who kills that which he does not devour, and this quality makes him so much a benefactor to our species."

'"If men kill our prey and lay it in our way," said the young one, "what need shall we have of labouring for ourselves?"

' "Because man will, sometimes," replied the mother, "remain for a long time quiet in his den. The old vultures will tell you when you are to watch his motions. When you see men in great numbers moving close together, like a flight of storks, you may conclude that they are hunting, and that you will soon revel in human blood."

' "But still," said the young one, "I would gladly know the reason of this mutual slaughter. I could never kill what I could not eat."

' "My child," said the mother, "this is a question which I cannot answer, though I am reckoned the most subtle bird of the mountain. When I was young I used frequently to visit the eyrie of an old vulture who dwelt upon the Carpathian rocks; he had made many observations; he knew the places that afforded prey round his habitation, as far in every direction as the strongest wing can fly between the rising and setting of the summer sun; he had fed year after year on the entrails of men. His opinion was that men had only the appearance of animal life, being really vegetables with a power of motion; and that as the boughs of an oak are dashed together by the storm, that swine may fatten upon the falling acorns, so men are by some unaccountable power driven one against another, till they lose their motion, that vultures may be fed. Others think they have observed something of contrivance and policy among these mischievous beings, and those that hover more closely round them pretend that there is, in every herd, one that gives directions to the rest, and seems to be more eminently delighted with a wide carnage. What it is that entitles him to such pre-eminence we know not; he is seldom the biggest or the swiftest, but he shows by his eagerness and diligence that he is, more than any of the others, a friend to vultures."'

Debtors' Prisons (1)

SIR,

As I was passing lately under one of the gates of this city, I was struck with horror by a rueful cry, which summoned me *to remember the poor Debtors*.

The wisdom and justice of the *English* laws are, by *Englishmen* at least, loudly celebrated; but scarcely the most zealous admirers of our Institutions can think that law wise, which when men are capable of work, obliges them to beg; or just, which exposes the liberty of one to the passions of another.

The prosperity of a people is proportionate to the number of hands and minds usefully employed. To the community sedition is a fever, corruption is a gangrene, and idleness an atrophy. Whatever body, and whatever society, wastes more than it acquires, must gradually decay; and every being that continues to be fed, and ceases to labour, takes away something from the public stock.

The confinement, therefore, of any man in the sloth and darkness of a prison, is a loss to the nation, and no gain to the Creditor. For of the multitudes who are pining in those cells of misery, a very small part is suspected of any fraudulent act by which they retain what belongs to others. The rest are imprisoned by the

109

wantonness of pride, the malignity of revenge, or the acrimony of disappointed expectation.

If those, who thus rigorously exercise the power which the law has put into their hands, be asked, why they continue to imprison those whom they know to be unable to pay them: One will answer, that his Debtor once lived better than himself; another, that his wife looked above her neighbours, and his children went in silk cloaths to the dancing school; and another, that he pretended to be a joker and a wit. Some will reply, that if they were in debt they should meet with the same treatment; some, that they owe no more than they can pay, and need therefore give no account of their actions. Some will confess their resolution, that their Debtors shall rot in jail; and some will discover, that they hope, by cruelty, to wring the payment from their friends.

The end of all civil regulations is to secure private happiness from private malignity; to keep individuals from the power of one another; but this end is apparently neglected, when a man, irritated with loss, is allowed to be the judge of his own cause, and to assign the punishment of his own pain; when the distinction between guilt and unhappiness, between casualty and design, is intrusted to eyes blind with interest, to understandings depraved by resentment.

Since Poverty is punished among us as a crime, it ought at least to be treated with the same lenity as other crimes; the offender ought not to languish, at the will of him whom he has offended, but to be allowed some appeal to the justice of his country. There can be no reason, why any Debtor should be imprisoned, but that he may be compelled to payment; and a term should therefore be fixed, in which the Creditor should exhibit his accusation of concealed property. If such property can be discovered, let it be given to the Creditor; if the charge is not offered, or cannot be proved, let the prisoner be dismissed.

Those who made the laws, have apparently supposed, that every deficiency of payment is the crime of the Debtor. But the truth is, that the Creditor always shares the act, and often more than shares the guilt of improper trust. It seldom happens that any man imprisons another but for debts which he suffered to be contracted, in hope of advantage to himself, and for bargains in which he proportioned his profit to his own opinion of the hazard; and there is no reason, why one should punish the other, for a contract in which both concurred.

Many of the inhabitants of prisons may justly complain of harder treatment. He that once owes more than he can pay, is often obliged to bribe his Creditor to patience, by encreasing his debt. Worse and worse commodities, at a higher and higher price, are forced upon him; he is impoverished by compulsive traffick, and at last over-whelmed, in the common receptacles of misery, by debts, which, without his own consent, were accumulated on his head. To the relief of this distress, no other objection can be made, but that by an easy dissolution of debts, fraud will be left without punishment, and imprudence without awe, and that when insolvency shall be no longer punishable, credit will cease.

The motive to credit, is the hope of advantage. Commerce can never be at a stop, while one man wants what another can supply; and credit will never be denied, while it is likely to be repaid with profit. He that trusts one whom he designs to sue, is criminal by the act of trust; the cessation of such insidious traffick is to be desired, and no reason can be given why a change of the law should impair any other.

We see nation trade with nation, where no payment can be compelled. Mutual convenience produces mutual confidence, and the Merchants continue to satisfy the demands of each other, though they have nothing to dread but the loss of trade.

It is vain to continue an institution, which experience shews to be ineffectual. We have now imprisoned one generation of Debtors after another, but we do not find that their numbers lessen. We have now learned, that rashness and imprudence will not be deterred from taking credit; let us try whether fraud and avarice may be more easily restrained from giving it.

I am, Sir, &c.

Consolation in the Face of Death

The following Letter relates to an affliction perhaps not necessary to be imparted to the Publick, but I could not persuade myself to suppress it, because I think I know the sentiments to be sincere, and I feel no disposition to provide for this day any other entertainment.

> *At tu quisquis eris, miseri qui cruda poetæ*
> *Credideris fletu funera digna tuo,*
> *Hæc postrema tibi sit flendi causa, fluatque*
> *Lenis inoffenso vitaque morsque gradu.*

['But you, whoever you may be, you who thought the untimely death of an unhappy poet worthy of your tears; may this be your last time to weep, and may life and death for you flow smoothly on with an even pace.']

Mr. IDLER,

Notwithstanding the warnings of Philosophers, and the daily examples of losses and misfortunes which life forces upon our observation, such is the absorption of our thoughts in the business of the present day, such the resignation of our reason to empty hopes of future felicity, or such our unwillingness to foresee what we dread, that every calamity comes suddenly upon us, and not only presses us as a burthen, but crushes as a blow.

There are evils which happen out of the common course of nature, against which it is no reproach not to be provided. A flash of lightning intercepts the traveller in his way. The concussion of an earthquake heaps the ruins of cities upon their inhabitants. But other miseries time brings, though silently yet visibly forward by its even lapse, which yet approach us unseen because we turn our eyes away, and seize us unresisted because we could not arm ourselves against them, but by setting them before us.

That it is vain to shrink from what cannot be avoided, and to hide that from ourselves which must some time be found, is a truth which we all know, but which all neglect, and perhaps none more than the speculative reasoner, whose thoughts are always from home, whose eye wanders over life, whose fancy dances after meteors of happiness kindled by itself, and who examines every thing rather than his own state.

Nothing is more evident than that the decays of age must terminate in death; yet there is no man, says *Tully*, who does not believe that he may yet live another year; and there is none who does not, upon the same principle, hope another year for his parent or his friend; but the fallacy will be in time detected; the last year, the last day must come. It has come and is past. The life which made my own life pleasant is at an end, and the gates of death are shut upon my prospects.

The loss of a friend upon whom the heart was fixed, to whom every wish and endeavour tended, is a state of dreary desolation in which the mind looks abroad impatient of itself, and finds nothing but emptiness and horror. The blameless life, the artless tenderness, the pious simplicity, the modest resignation, the patient sickness, and the quiet death, are remembered only to add value to the loss, to aggravate regret for what cannot be amended, to deepen sorrow for what cannot be recalled.

These are the calamities by which Providence gradually disengages us from the love of life. Other evils fortitude may repel, or hope may mitigate; but irreparable privation leaves nothing to exercise resolution or flatter expectation. The dead cannot return, and nothing is left us here but languishment and grief.

Yet such is the course of nature, that whoever lives long must outlive those whom he loves and honours. Such is the condition of our present existence, that life must one time lose its associations, and every inhabitant of the earth must walk downward to the grave alone and unregarded, without any partner of his joy or grief, without any interested witness of his misfortunes or success.

Misfortune, indeed, he may yet feel, for where is the bottom of the misery of man? But what is success to him that has none to enjoy it. Happiness is not found in self-contemplation; it is perceived only when it is reflected from another.

We know little of the state of departed souls, because such knowledge is not necessary to a good life. Reason deserts us at the brink of the grave, and can give no further intelligence. Revelation is not wholly silent. *There is joy in the Angels of Heaven over one sinner that repenteth*; and surely this joy is not incommunicable to souls disentangled from the body, and made like Angels.

Let Hope therefore dictate, what Revelation does not confute, that the union of souls may still remain; and that we who are struggling with sin, sorrow, and infirmities, may have our part in the attention and kindness of those who have finished their course and are now receiving their reward.

These are the great occasions which force the mind to take refuge in Religion: when we have no help in ourselves, what can remain but that we look up to a higher and a greater Power; and to what hope may we not raise our eyes and hearts, when we consider that the Greatest POWER is the BEST.

Surely there is no man who, thus afflicted, does not seek succour in the *Gospel*, which has brought *Life and Immortality to light*. The Precepts of *Epicurus*, who teaches us to endure what the Laws of the Universe make necessary, may silence but not content us. The dictates of *Zeno*, who commands us to look with indifference on external things, may dispose us to conceal our sorrow, but cannot assuage it. Real alleviation of the loss of friends, and rational tranquillity in the prospect of our own dissolution, can be received only from the promises of him in whose hands are life and death, and from the assurance of another and better state, in which all tears will be wiped from the eyes, and the whole soul shall be filled with joy. Philosophy may infuse stubbornness, but Religion only can give Patience.

I am, &c.

The Nature of a Critic

Criticism is a study by which men grow important and formidable at very small expence. The power of invention has been conferred by Nature upon few, and the labour of learning those sciences which may, by mere labour, be obtained, is too great to be willingly endured; but every man can exert such judgment as he has upon the works of others; and he whom Nature has made weak, and Idleness keeps ignorant, may yet support his vanity by the name of a Critick.

I hope it will give comfort to great numbers who are passing thro' the world in obscurity, when I inform them how easily distinction may be obtained. All the other powers of literature are coy and haughty, they must be long courted, and at last are not always gained; but Criticism is a goddess easy of access and forward of advance, who will meet the slow and encourage the timorous; the want of meaning she supplies with words, and the want of spirit she recompenses with malignity.

This profession has one recommendation peculiar to itself, that it gives vent to malignity without real mischief. No genius was ever blasted by the breath of Criticks. The poison which, if confined, would have burst the heart, fumes away in empty hisses, and malice is set at ease with very little danger to merit. The Critick is the only man whose triumph is without another's pain, and whose greatness does not rise upon another's ruin.

To a study at once so easy and so reputable, so malicious and so harmless, it cannot be necessary to invite my readers by a long or laboured exhortation; it is sufficient, since all would be Criticks if they could, to shew by one eminent example that all can be Criticks if they will.

Dick Minim, after the common course of puerile studies, in which he was no great proficient, was put apprentice to a Brewer, with whom he had lived two years, when his uncle died in the city, and left him a large fortune in the stocks. *Dick* had for six months before used the company of the lower players, of whom he had learned to scorn a trade, and being now at liberty to follow his genius, he resolved to be a man of wit and humour. That he might be properly initiated in his new character, he frequented the coffee-houses near the theatres, where he listened very diligently day, after day, to those who talked of language and sentiments, and unities and catastrophes, till by slow degrees he began to think that he understood something of the Stage, and hoped in time to talk himself.

But he did not trust so much to natural sagacity, as wholly to neglect the help of books. When the theatres were shut, he retired to *Richmond* with a few select writers, whose opinions he impressed upon his memory by unwearied diligence; and when he returned with other wits to the town, was able to tell, in very proper phrases, that the chief business of art is to copy nature; that a perfect writer is not to be expected, because genius decays as judgment increases; that the great art is the art of blotting, and that according to the rule of *Horace* every piece should be kept nine years.

Of the great Authors he now began to display the Characters, laying down as an universal position that all had beauties and defects. His opinion was, that *Shakespear*, committing himself wholly to the impulse of Nature, wanted that correctness which learning would have given him; and that *Johnson*, trusting to learning, did not sufficiently cast his eye on Nature. He blamed the *Stanza* of *Spenser*, and could not bear the *Hexameters* of *Sidney*. *Denham* and *Waller* he held the first reformers of *English* Numbers, and thought that if *Waller* could have obtained the strength of *Denham*, or *Denham* the sweetness of *Waller*, there had been nothing wanting to complete a Poet. He often expressed his commiseration of *Dryden*'s poverty, and his indignation at the age which suffered him to write for bread; he repeated with rapture the first lines of *All for Love*, but wondered at the corruption of taste which could bear any thing so unnatural as rhyming Tragedies. In *Otway* he found uncommon powers of moving the passions, but was disgusted by his general negligence, and blamed him for making a Conspirator his Hero; and never concluded his disquisition, without remarking how happily the sound of the clock is made to alarm the audience. *Southern* would have been his favourite, but that he mixes comick with tragick scenes, intercepts the natural course of the passions, and fills the mind with a wild confusion of mirth and melancholy. The versification of *Rowe* he thought too melodious for the stage, and too little varied in different passions. He made it the great fault of *Congreve*, that all his persons were wits, and that he always wrote with more art than nature. He considered *Cato* rather as a poem than a play, and allowed *Addison* to be the complete master of Allegory and grave humour, but paid no great deference to him as a Critick. He thought the chief merit of *Prior* was in his easy tales and lighter poems, tho' he allowed that his *Solomon* had many noble sentiments elegantly expressed. In *Swift* he discovered an inimitable vein of irony, and an easiness which all would hope and few would attain. *Pope* he was inclined to degrade from a Poet to a Versifier, and thought his Numbers rather luscious than sweet. He often lamented the neglect of *Phædra and Hippolitus*, and wished to see the stage under better regulations.

These assertions passed commonly uncontradicted; and if now and then an opponent started up, he was quickly repressed by the suffrages of the company, and *Minim* went away from every dispute with elation of heart and increase of confidence.

He now grew conscious of his abilities, and began to talk of the present state of dramatick Poetry; wondered what was become of the comick genius which supplied our ancestors with wit and pleasantry, and why no writer could be found that durst now venture beyond a Farce. He saw no reason for thinking that the vein of humour was exhausted, since we live in a country where liberty suffers every character to spread itself to its utmost bulk, and which therefore produces more originals than all the rest of the world together. Of Tragedy he concluded business to be the soul, and yet often hinted that love predominates too much upon the modern stage.

He was now an acknowledged Critick, and had his own seat in the coffee-house, and headed a party in the pit. *Minim* has more vanity than ill-nature, and seldom desires to do much mischief; he will perhaps murmur a little in the ear of him that sits next him, but endeavours to influence the audience to favour, by clapping when an actor exclaims *ye Gods*, or laments the misery of his country.

By degrees he was admitted to Rehearsals, and many of his friends are of opinion, that our present Poets are indebted to him for their happiest thoughts; by his contrivance the bell was rung twice in *Barbarossa*, and by his persuasion the author of *Cleone* concluded his Play without a couplet; for what can be more absurd, said *Minim*, than that part of a play should be rhymed, and part written in blank verse? and by what acquisition of faculties is the Speaker who never could find rhymes before, enabled to rhyme at the conclusion of an Act!

He is the great investigator of hidden beauties, and is particularly delighted when he finds *the Sound an Echo to the Sense*. He has read all our Poets with particular attention to this delicacy of Versification, and wonders at the supineness with which their Works have been hitherto perused, so that no man has found the sound of a Drum in this distich,

> When Pulpit, Drum ecclesiastic,
> Was beat with fist instead of a stick,

and that the wonderful lines upon Honour and a Bubble
have hitherto passed without notice.

> Honour is like the glassy Bubble,
> Which costs Philosophers such trouble,
> Where one part crack'd, the whole does fly,
> And Wits are crack'd to find out why.

In these Verses, says *Minim*, we have two striking accom-
modations of the Sound to the Sense. It is impossible to
utter the two lines emphatically without an act like
that which they describe; *Bubble* and *Trouble* causing a
momentary inflation of the Cheeks by the retention of
the breath, which is afterwards forcibly emitted, as in
the practice of *blowing bubbles*. But the greatest excellence
is in the third line, which is *crack'd* in the middle to
express a crack, and then shivers into monosyllables. Yet
has this diamond lain neglected with common stones,
and among the innumerable admirers of *Hudibras* the
observation of this superlative passage has been reserved
for the sagacity of *Minim*.

European Oppression in America

As the *English* army was passing towards *Quebec* along a soft savanna between a mountain and a lake, one of the petty Chiefs of the inland regions stood upon a rock surrounded by his clan, and from behind the shelter of the bushes contemplated the art and regularity of *European* war. It was evening, the tents were pitched, he observed the security with which the troops rested in the night, and the order with which the march was renewed in the morning. He continued to pursue them with his eye till they could be seen no longer, and then stood for some time silent and pensive.

Then turning to his followers, 'My children (said he) I have often heard from men hoary with long life, that there was a time when our ancestors were absolute lords of the woods, the meadows, and the lakes, wherever the eye can reach or the foot can pass. They fished and hunted, feasted and danced, and when they were weary lay down under the first thicket, without danger and without fear. They changed their habitations as the seasons required, convenience prompted, or curiosity allured them, and sometimes gathered the fruits of the mountain, and sometimes sported in canoes along the coast.

'Many years and ages are supposed to have been thus passed in plenty and security; when at last, a new race

of men entered our country from the great Ocean. They
inclosed themselves in habitations of stone, which our
ancestors could neither enter by violence, nor destroy
by fire. They issued from those fastnesses, sometimes
covered like the armadillo with shells, from which the
lance rebounded on the striker, and sometimes carried
by mighty beasts which had never been seen in our
vales or forests, of such strength and swiftness, that flight
and opposition were vain alike. Those invaders ranged
over the continent, slaughtering in their rage those
that resisted, and those that submitted, in their mirth.
Of those that remained, some were buried in caverns,
and condemned to dig metals for their masters; some
were employed in tilling the ground, of which foreign
tyrants devour the produce; and when the sword and
the mines have destroyed the natives, they supply their
place by human beings of another colour, brought from
some distant country to perish here under toil and
torture.

'Some there are who boast their humanity, and content themselves to seize our chaces and fisheries, who
drive us from every track of ground where fertility
and pleasantness invite them to settle, and make no
war upon us except when we intrude upon our own
lands.

'Others pretend to have purchased a right of residence
and tyranny; but surely the insolence of such bargains is
more offensive than the avowed and open dominion of
force. What reward can induce the possessor of a country
to admit a stranger more powerful than himself? Fraud
or terror must operate in such contracts; either they

promised protection which they never have afforded, or instruction which they never imparted. We hoped to be secured by their favour from some other evil, or to learn the arts of *Europe*, by which we might be able to secure ourselves. Their power they have never exerted in our defence, and their arts they have studiously concealed from us. Their treaties are only to deceive, and their traffick only to defraud us. They have a written Law among them, of which they boast as derived from him who made the Earth and Sea, and by which they profess to believe that man will be made happy when life shall forsake him. Why is not this Law communicated to us? It is concealed because it is violated. For how can they preach it to an *Indian* nation, when I am told that one of its first precepts forbids them to do to others what they would not that others should do to them.

'But the time perhaps is now approaching when the pride of usurpation shall be crushed, and the cruelties of invasion shall be revenged. The Sons of Rapacity have now drawn their swords upon each other, and referred their claims to the decision of war; let us look unconcerned upon the slaughter, and remember that the death of every *European* delivers the country from a tyrant and a robber; for what is the claim of either nation, but the claim of the vultur to the leveret, of the tiger to the faun? Let them then continue to dispute their title to regions which they cannot people, to purchase by danger and blood the empty dignity of dominion over mountains which they will never climb, and rivers which they will never pass. Let us endeavour, in the mean time, to learn their discipline, and to forge their weapons; and when they shall be weakened with mutual slaughter, let us rush down upon them, force their remains to take shelter in their ships, and reign once more in our native country.'

THE STORY OF PENGUIN CLASSICS

Before 1946 ...'Classics' are mainly the domain of academics and students, without readable editions for everyone else. This all changes when a little-known classicist, E. V. Rieu, presents Penguin founder Allen Lane with the translation of Homer's Odyssey that he has been working on and reading to his wife Nelly in his spare time.

1946 The Odyssey becomes the first Penguin Classic published, and promptly sells three million copies. Suddenly, classic books are no longer for the privileged few.

1950s Rieu, now series editor, turns to professional writers for the best modern, readable translations, including Dorothy L. Sayers's *Inferno* and Robert Graves's *The Twelve Caesars*, which revives the salacious original.

1960s 1961 sees the arrival of the Penguin Modern Classics, showcasing the best twentieth-century writers from around the world. Rieu retires in 1964, hailing the Penguin Classics list as 'the greatest educative force of the 20th century'.

1970s A new generation of translators arrives to swell the Penguin Classics ranks, and the list grows to encompass more philosophy, religion, science, history and politics.

1980s The Penguin American Library joins the Classics stable, with titles such as *The Last of the Mohicans* safeguarded. Penguin Classics now offers the most comprehensive library of world literature available.

1990s Penguin Popular Classics are launched, offering readers budget editions of the greatest works of literature. Penguin Audiobooks brings the classics to a listening audience for the first time, and in 1999 the launch of the Penguin Classics website takes them online to an ever larger global readership.

The 21st Century Penguin Classics are rejacketed for the first time in nearly twenty years. This world famous series now consists of more than 1,300 titles, making the widest range of the best books ever written available to millions – and constantly redefining the meaning of what makes a 'classic'.

The Odyssey continues ...

The best books ever written

PENGUIN 🐧 CLASSICS

SINCE 1946

Find out more at www.penguinclassics.com